Nearly, But Not Quite

Lloyd Hodkinson

INDEX

Introduction 5

Early years 7

The Kibworth Years 1955 – 61 13

Ashover Road 1961 27

Knighton Church Road 1963 - 67 35

HMS Fisgard 1967 - 68 49

HMS Caledonia 1969 - 71 61

HMS Jaguar 1971 - 72 73

HMS Hermes 1973-75 91

Leaving the RN 1975 -79 97

Ross on Wye 1980 - 85 105

MV Doulos in the Med 1985 113

Doulos in West Africa 1986 131

A passage to India and beyond 1987 147

Bromley, Urmston to Bolton 1987 - 90 157

Stamford 1991 - 99 165

CLC Alresford 1999 - 2003 173

CLC International – Sheffield 2003 - 2006 179

Tillicoultry - The End of the Road? 2017 – 189

Nearly but not quite 193

INTRODUCTION

I have always wanted to start a book; with "I was born at an early age". Or "on my birthday I was found in the arms of another man's wife, my mother", but that is just too trite. I thought about starting with "my first memory was …" but that is just as bad. So now having written a few lines I have already started and can just get on with the job.

It would have been good to have started this book a few years ago when my parents were both still alive and then I may have got some of the details right and my mother could have corrected my grammar and spelling.

One of the problems I have found of writing an autobiography is that in the process one recalls incidents etc. that are from a period about which one has already written. Also, I found, that some aspects of one's life cannot easily be recorded in a linear chronological format. To try and retain the readers' interest I have done some in chronological order and interspersed it with other relevant information.

So much of my story and life is due to the influences that others had on my life, the most significant of these was probably my Father, I have included some information about him, as part of my story.

Disclaimer

The following writings are from my aged memory. It may be correct or incorrect or even fiction. It is up to you to decide which.

Chapter 1

EARLY YEARS

From the things I remember of what I was told. My maternal grandparents lived in Salford, Lancashire - near to Manchester for those not familiar with English geography. In the 1990's I went to see the house my mother grew up in and was surprised to find that it was quite affluent in its day but now is well past its former glory. Grandfather was a sales representative for a cotton manufacturer, and the family were able to afford a live in maid to help with the housework. Unfortunately, in the 1920's the cotton industry in Manchester collapsed and in due time Grandfather moved to the city of Leicester, where he became a clerk for the government and the family lived in considerably reduced circumstances.

On my father's side my Grandfather, who I never knew, lived in Woking. After war service in Mesopotamia, where he contracted TB, Grandfather had, for health reasons, moved to work as a gardener for a country house in Leicestershire. By the early twenties he had passed away and Grandma with two boys and a girl was living in the gatehouse of Kibworth Hall just outside Leicester. My father's uncle, who had emigrated to Canada, offered to take one of the boys to help bring him up. The family story is that Uncle Jack (the oldest son) was due to travel, but for some reason, we were told he was naughty, he did not travel but my father travelled alone from rural Leicestershire to Toronto in Canada, I understand at the age of 12. It is more likely that as Uncle Jack was 14 years of age he would be working and able to bring some income into the household.

We will come back to stories of Kibworth later in this narrative. Meanwhile Father grew up in Canada and trained in bookkeeping and accountancy. In the early 30's he decided to travel back to England to see his mother. He met my mother and in due time they married and had our family.

My father and mother were, as were both sets of grandparents, members of a small denomination of Christians known as "the Brethren". Much has been written about the Brethren and some of the many variations of the denomination which can be extremely exclusive and even cultish in places. The branch of the group my parents were associated with would be described as fundamentalist non-conformist Christians, but as they were an autonomous church they were influenced but not controlled by others outside of the church. The Open Brethren as they were often described have been responsible for more missionary activity per head of membership than any other single denomination. And many of the leaders of the new wave of Charismatic House Church movement of the 60's and 70's came out of the Brethren movement. What this meant for us as a family was that we had quite an active and happy childhood but restricted in what we were allowed to do and who we were allowed to mix with. Most of our activities and entertainment came from within the church and its membership.

My father was conscripted into the Army during WW2. He was, because of his beliefs, a conscientious objector and was sent into the Pioneer Corp. This was basically a labour force whose primary task was digging trenches, etc. They were often ordered to dig out debris so that bomb disposal officers could get at unexploded bombs, they were considered expendable. After some time my father transferred to the Royal Army Medical Corps and spent the remainder of the war near the frontline working in emergency aid stations. His unit were parachute trained and also deployed in gliders. I attended his unit reunion with him some years later and found out that he had on several occasions been recommended for gallantry awards for saving lives. But the official opinion was that you couldn't give a conscientious objector a gallantry award because they were considered cowards. Thankfully we now live in more enlightened days.

After the war Dad returned to live in Leicester with Mum and the family. He had a job in Kibworth ten miles outside Leicester and used to ride his bicycle to work and back every day come rain come shine. The family lived in Stratford Road. My brothers: Mervyn (born 1938), Alan (born 1941), and my sister Ruth (born 1944), had their peace shattered, when on 7th September 1950, I, Lloyd George Hodkinson arrived on the scene, born at Leicester General Hospital; I have no memory of the event.

My earliest memory is watching the coronation on a TV at a church friend's home, now if I can really remember or remember being told about it, I am not sure, but around that year we moved to 200 Braunstone Lane, in Leicester. It was a typical three-bedroom semi-detached house, I have no memory of the inside of it at all. It was really useful to me some years later, when I was being bullied at school and I found out that the bully lived in Braunstone; I was able to convince him that I also came from that area and so should be exempt from his bullying. It worked for a while until he started going round his old victims again.

I think that by this time Mervyn had started to work on British Rail. During the time we lived at Braunstone Lane I was taken to Mildmay Mission Hospital in London to have my tonsils removed. My mother took me on the train and I can still remember being left for a week and mother coming to take me home again. Mother used to tell the story that I didn't even notice but I can remember it very clearly as the longest cup of tea she ever had with the sister.

I was outside playing one day in the rain, wearing my red mackintosh when a man passing by told me that my parents couldn't care for me as they let me out to play in the rain. We lived just a few yards from an old inn and during my time there I remember the place was developed and they built a big car park. I used to walk along the road and watch the workmen and even sometimes got a biscuit from them when they had their tea breaks. Many would not allow children to play out like that these days for fear of paedophiles.

Mother had a routine that she kept up for many years. After lunch she would listen to Woman's Hour on the radio and sit and do her knitting, during that period she was NOT to be disturbed. It was here that I learnt that "the look" was almost as bad as the punishment, without saying a word she could look over the top of her glasses and reduce the whole family to silence. When that programme finished was the start of Children's Hour and mother would start to prepare the family evening meal.

We used to live close to one side of a large public park called Braunstone Park and my mother's parents lived on the other side so fairly regularly we walked across and had lunch with the grandparents. I used to think that grandma was quite odd because she made custard that was thin and almost white and served it from a bowl, whilst at our house we had yellow custard from a jug. They also used to get cakes from the electric baker's van that travelled around as well as Gingernut Buttons. These were smaller than regular biscuits and came loose in a white paper bag. Of such are the memories of children.

It was at Braunstone Lane that I met "Twinkie". It must have been love at first sight. Who couldn't love a bright blue tricycle with a white basket on the front and a box on the back with a closing lid. I used to go everywhere on Twinkie, and what was even better was when my brother Alan used to get on the back and scoot me along at speeds approaching Mach 1.

We used to go to Sunday school on Sunday afternoon, The Sunday school was so popular at that time that it was too big for the church, so some classes were held in a local primary school. My only real memory was being told to close my eyes when the prayers were being said. I thought it was because God hid behind the curtains on the stage and came out when all the eyes were closed because he was so awesome that people couldn't look at him, and he wouldn't come if anyone had their eyes open.

Then one day my father took me, and the tea set in a cardboard box, on the train back to Kibworth. It was safer for Dad to carry the tea set than to risk it in the removal van. The removal men had promised that if they couldn't get Twinkie into the van, they had a piece of string and would tow Twinkie behind. And so, we moved to Kibworth. I was not yet five years old.

Chapter 2

THE KIBWORTH YEARS 1955 – 61

The house we moved into was a large Victorian Villa with three floors, four bedrooms, and even a breakfast room as well as a drawing room and a dining room.

I guess that Dad had got a promotion at work or something because the house was owned by the company. England was still coming to terms with the end of the war and the 50's were known as the austerity years. Because we lived in a company house, I don't think Dad got as much money as he would have if he lived in his own house. Having said that, by comparison with many others, we were quite comfortable. One drawback was the very small garden, but Dad soon took two very large allotments and grew most of our vegetables on his allotments.

Mother was not a well lady with unspecified illnesses to us little children, so Mrs Calvert came to help with the cleaning two or three days a week. She was wonderful treating me just like one of her own boys, she used to threaten to suck my toys up the vacuum cleaner. She became a friend of the family and many years after she should have retired, she would come to the house and have a "run around with the duster" as she used to say. The tea breaks with my mother expanded to being greater than the work done.

We moved in mid-summer, and it seemed every day was sunshine. I could ride Twinkie up and down the paths in front of our house and walk with Dad to help (hinder) on the allotments, I could run around to my heart's content. Then in September, I started school, the fear of going into the playground alone on the first day was sufficient to bring tears. But very soon we were in a classroom, about 35 of us who progressed through the village schools together. I sat next to another boy who wore glasses, this was unusual in those days at that age. But Mum and Dad had told me that if I was kind to someone, I might make a friend. John was even more frightened in the playground than I was, so it was easy to be kind to him, we just had to stand together. John Allen became my best friend. When we were given tasks to copy from the blackboard he used to copy from my paper, because he could see that. It took both of us a long time to write our "S" correctly, I used to do them reversed and he used to copy. This was how the teachers really identified his problems. He was partially sighted and after a few years moved to a special school for Blind and partially sighted children. Our friendship continued for many years, even after that.

Our teacher was Miss Bale, and the head mistress was Mrs Henderson. I imagine that my years at infant school were reasonably happy as I have very few real memories of those days, except the play times and other fun activities like Maypole dancing. I think that was the last time I enjoyed dancing, and probably only because I was allowed to partner Pat Welton the Junior school headmaster's daughter. She was the belle of the school and the leader of the gang of females. In my experience there is always one kid in every class who got the plum parts in school plays, etc. She was that kid, but it did mean if you were part of the group that you could bask in reflected glory.

Kibworth was wonderful. But I was a sickly child and spent several extended periods in hospital, in "isolation" wards. Memories are hazy about those days, perhaps because I was not well. Our doctor was Dr Barker. He treated me for all the childhood ailments, whooping cough, measles, German measles, chicken pox and so on but when I was about seven, he made a suggestion that changed things considerably. I was to be allowed to go camping with Dad. He said the fresh air would do me good. It either worked or I had run out of illnesses to have.

My father helped run, an annual camp for boys, that was supported by the Church we attended. It took place for one week in August each year. 1957 was the first year it was held on the farm owned by the "Stanleys'" at Eastwell, Leicestershire. The camp used a field and set up a camp, several marques and sleeping tents. The toilets were a pit in the corner and meals tended to be heavy on potatoes and beans and light on fancy items. Games were organised every day between various teams. And everyone was given a good dose of evangelical gospel teaching twice a day, with the intention of getting as many boys "saved" as possible. It sounds horrendous now to modern thinking but was typical of its time. The committee who ran the camp did over the years try to keep up with the times. The camp was set on top of a ridge of hills overlooking the Vale of Belvoir (pronounced Beever) and was a most beautiful setting. Many of the boys who came as much as twenty miles from surrounding cities had never really seen such a nice place and had such good care. I remember one boy crying because he didn't want to go home, not just because he had been having a good time, but because he knew it was better than he would get at home. One difficulty with the camp site was its exposed position on the hilltop and one evening whilst we were having our tea the wind blew and broke the ridge pole of the marquee. The wind also slipped the couplings on another tent causing it to collapse. I also have memories of leaders walking around during the night hammering in tent pegs to keep the tents up in the poor weather. But in the best of British tradition, we had a great time.

Some of my most persistent memories from this period were playing with John. His family lived on the other side of the village, but quite regularly I would walk home with John or he would come with me after school. We would play with Dinky Toys most often. Mine were a mixture of lorries, cars and military vehicles with a sprinkling of ship models, even in those days. John predominantly had farm toys. His father at the time was an itinerant farm labourer who had just invested in a small holding hoping to build it up into a farm as a future employment for John. When we visited John's house, we nearly always finished with a trip up the road to check the animals and do the chores. I was probably helping feed pigs before I could read. We also used to play at Cowboys and Indians in their garden. This occasionally included tying Jane, John's sister, to a convenient tree with a skipping rope and pretending to rescue her from the baddies. This was a good game until on one occasion, having tied her up, we got distracted into playing a different game with the boys across the road and forgot to release her. We certainly got into trouble for that and perhaps that is why, when some fifteen years later, I asked her out on a date she declined.

During the summer holidays I would often spend full days with John and his family. We would be taken to help on different farms with the harvesting. The farmers with the labourers used to work together harvesting on one farm then moving to the next farm and so on. There may have been as many as twenty men working in one field during haymaking. During school holidays there would be quite a number of children and a hierarchy soon developed with the oldest, who could drive a tractor, being at the top, being on a trailer was next highest with hayrick building only being allowed on the farm, if you lived there. John and I were fairly low in the pecking order, until we were allowed and taught how to drive the tractor at the age of eight. John became an expert but couldn't see where he was going until he got close up, anything over a couple of yards was a foggy mist, so I used to sit beside him and direct operations. In later years on his own family farm, he could drive around and find his way, by the feel of the land as he drove across it.

The farmer's wife used to bring out lunch for the workers and I can still taste some of the cheese and pickle sandwiches that were the mainstay of lunch. But what we boys really wanted and waited for was the rich fruit cake served with a slice of Red Leicester cheese. I didn't like the fruit cake and John didn't like the cheese, so that was another good reason to be friends.

After three years of intensive schooling, aged seven it was time to graduate to the junior school. Kibworth C of E Junior School was in those days housed in a Victorian building, still standing on Station Road, Kibworth. It was a large open building at some point divided by partitions into smaller classrooms, but one had to pass through each classroom to move from place to place as there were no corridors. The building was heated by large pot- bellied coke heaters in each room with a huge guard around them like a garden fence, complete with gate to allow the caretaker access to top up with fuel several times a day. The windows in a Gothic style were so high that even adults could not see in or out. It was grim building at age seven. The playground was in two parts and classes 1 & 2 used one and 3 & 4 the other. But the boy's toilets were an outbuilding in year 3 & 4 yard and the girls in the other, so one took one's life in one's own hands if you needed to use the facility during a break period.

They had an interesting, by today's standards, method of getting a drink of water; attached to the wash hand basin at the toilets, outdoor, no hot water, was a large industrial spoon. A child was expected to turn on the tap and fill the spoon with water and take a drink from it and turn off the tap and leave the spoon for the next person. I don't think the spoon was ever cleaned properly and childhood illnesses and infections ran through the school time after time.

I was astounded on my first day at junior school. Miss Gardner was the Year 1 teacher and feared by almost everyone in the village. As we walked in she asked me how my Uncle John was? I replied, "I don't have an Uncle John". "Yes you do", she said and that was the end of that conversation. A little later she asked me again and also asked me how my father, Henry, was getting on. This threw me into total confusion, as I didn't at that stage realise my Dad had a name other than Dad but I did know some people called him Frank. When I got home this was an instant point to bring up with Mum. She had to explain that Dad had a name, Henry Frank Hodkinson, and that his brother John Hodkinson was known to me as Uncle Jack.

Miss Gardner had taught both my uncle and father in the 1920's in that same classroom. During the year I was in her class the school moved to a modern building and Miss Gardner moved into a different classroom for the only time in her career. When she eventually retired, she had only ever taught seven year olds, first year juniors at the same school. She had in some cases taught, grandparents, parents and children of the same family.

As an old-fashioned teacher, some of Miss Gardner's methods would be considered awful by today's teachers but she certainly managed to get us all coping with the three "R's" Reading, Writing and Arithmetic.

Every Friday afternoon we had an Arithmetic test of 20 questions and a spelling test of 20 words, followed by a reading test by each pupil individually. Whilst the reading test was going on we were allowed the only "Art" lesson of the week when we were told to draw something or other or make patterns or something. Then came the big moment when we moved desk. These were the big iron framed double desks with a lift up bench for two. If you had achieved between 30 and 40 marks in the test you were moved into aisle A with the highest mark at the back, 30 to 20 were in aisle B and 20 and below in aisle C and the punishment row was aisle D.

Aisle A was regularly made up of the same group, Lloyd Hodkinson, Pat Welton, Beverly Burrows, Janet Scott, Hilary Bolton, Helen Gamble and so on. The problem was that only occasionally did Andrew Newton make it onto Aisle A. Andrew's family emigrated to USA a few years later. The last I heard he had graduated as an Officer in the US Coast Guard Corps. Otherwise I was the only boy. This led to me learning that there are some things you do not even confide to your mother. Having told my mother I didn't like being the only boy in that row, she then told

Miss Gardner!! Miss Gardner then made great play out of moving me from Row A to Row D until I learnt there was nothing wrong with being clever!! I never have understood her logic. It was sitting with the seven-year-old girls I didn't like.

Like most children in those years, I had school dinners. The meals were subsidised by the government to ensure that all children got at least one good hot meal a day. As a school we had to walk in line around the corner into the dining room of the Infant School to get dinner. We sat on long tables with a teacher at the end to keep order and ensure we ate what was put in front of us. I was fortunate that my parents had taught us to eat most things and enjoy them, but I still have sympathy for children who are forced to eat something they really do not like. I gained a real dislike for Semolina and Rice pudding during this period and still find it almost impossible to eat.

After we had eaten, whilst others were finishing, Miss Gardner would call one or another to come and stand beside her to recite the times tables from 2 to 12. Many was the small boy or girl who got their calves slapped for not knowing what 7 x 6 was or something similar. But Oh the joy for those of us who managed to get to 12 x 12 = 144 because Miss Gardner would dip her hand into her capacious handbag and produce a stick of Barley Sugar.

After she retired, my mother met Miss Gardner in the street and told her that I had got the equivalent of a degree in Naval Engineering. There was no congratulation but a sharp "Not before Time". I wish my children had been taught by Miss Gardner.

That same year the school moved into modern premises just out of the centre of the village, but to us children nothing really changed. We had the same teachers teaching the same things in the same old way.

John had changed school and travelled into Leicester every day so other friends appeared from time to time and sometimes adventures happened solo.

By this time, I had graduated from "Twinkie" to a proper bicycle. I remember teaching myself to balance on it by riding along the narrow passageway at the side of the house and scraping my knees and elbows against the brickwork instead of falling off completely. Riding the bike added a number of extra dimensions to play and activities. I was allowed to ride anywhere in the village but not to go past the 30 MPH signs. Being a good boy, this led to me travelling several hundred yards round the backstreets of one part of the village because the "30" signs at one crossroad meant there was a six foot section that was outside the area. The village was quite large so was almost a mile from our house to the furthest point, which was a long way for a small boy. On one occasion I decided to go to the limit on a hot sunny afternoon, arriving at the far end I realised I had a flat tyre. Out came my little tyre pump and I set to, trying to get it pumped up to ride home. At this point the village policeman, PC Dare, (his daughter Patricia was in my class at school) drove past in his Morris Minor travelling out of town. Sometime later when I was crying with frustration at not being able pump up the tyre, PC Dare drove back into town and stopped to see if I was alright, and in a gesture, unheard of these days, took me into custody sitting me in the front of the car and putting my bicycle into the boot. He then drove me home and released me into the care of my mother. He reinforced for me in those early years, the same thing that my parents taught, that the police are actually there to help law abiding citizens.

For most of the time we lived at Kibworth, my oldest brother Mervyn lived in lodgings in Leicester. He was working for British Rail involved with the signalling. But above all he was my Big Brother. I thought that there was nothing that he couldn't do. But I started to realise that sometimes he would rather be with the youth group and one girl in particular, than with me. I noticed this when she came to stay with us some weekends. And it became apparent that I was a lost cause when they got engaged, I didn't like Beryl much in those days. When they got married, they hired a coach to take the guests to Beryl's hometown where the wedding ceremony was taking place. Uncle Jack was the driver, and I was allowed to be the conductor. After we returned the coach Uncle Jack took me down into the inspection pit under a Double decker bus, happy memories.

Mervyn and Beryl put a lot of effort into helping me accept the situation. I think I was the first person to stay with them after they got married and we went on a number of trips, some local and two really memorable ones. Mervyn and I went by train to York and the National Rail Museum and a few other sites. And Mervyn, Beryl and I went to Birmingham, the highlight of which was Beryl choosing a new Sunday hat. Mervyn and I laughed so much that we were almost thrown out of C&A's. In fact, that memory was so strong that he and I talked about it and laughed again on the last occasion I saw him before he passed away.

Anecdote

During the summer holidays I was often a guest at John's parent's farm, whilst there I was treated just like their own kids and suffered the wrath of Mrs Allen just as much as John did. One day we had upset her during the lunch time and were banned from the farmhouse, but we wanted a drink. After several attempts at the kitchen door we asked Mr Allen what we should do. He advised that if we made a fire and boiled some water he would get us some tea and sugar from the larder. That sounded good to us. He told us there were some lopped branches in the orchard and found us a bucket to boil the water in. As we were both country boys it didn't take long to find a safe place to light a fire and get it going. We filled the bucket and set it over the fire on some bricks. Have you any idea how long it takes to boil a bucket of water? As we kept feeding the fire we gradually cleared all the orchard of branches (that saved Mr Allen a job) and it took quite a while to realise we should only heat the amount of water we actually wanted. Eventually we had boiled two cups of water and stirred in the tea and sugar. We strained the tea into cups through a handkerchief. And then looked at each other as we realised, we needed milk. Well, where do you get milk on a dairy farm? That's right, we backed a cow into the corner of a field, I held its head and John went under the back end with cup of tea in hand, Two squirts later and we were drinking our well-deserved tea. Just in time for evening milking and dinner.

Clear thinking can be so confusing

LH

Chapter 3

ASHOVER ROAD 1961

One day I was woken early to be told that my father had been arrested and taken to the police station. He had been accused by his company of embezzlement and false accounting. I was still only ten years old and did not understand all or even many of the details. I remember him coming home with Uncle Jack (his brother) and almost immediately going to bed, it seemed like it was for weeks. Mother was very tearful and everyone seemed sad. The story actually made it into the local evening paper and was the sensation of the village. The next day at school another boy in my class taunted me that my father was a thief. He immediately learnt what pain a straight right to the nose can be. There was blood everywhere, girls screamed, and someone fetched the headmaster. I was sent home for the rest of the week which didn't really help the situation.

In due time the case came to court and was not proven. This means that the prosecution failed to prove that my father was guilty and the case was dropped. I sometimes wish and I think Dad would have been happier if prosecution had completed their presentation and he had been found "Not Guilty". Some twenty years afterwards someone asked me if I thought he was or was not guilty. The person who asked very nearly learnt the pain of a straight right. All the while that this was going on our church kept faith with Dad and allowed him to continue as treasurer for the church a position he continued to hold until he retired. Anyone who really knew him would acknowledge that there was not a more honest man than Dad.

The upshot was that we could not stay in the company house where we were living, and Dad had to get a new job. A friend put him in touch with a clerical job that did not involve finance and so Dad spent the rest of his working life as a clerk counting lightbulb filaments. One of the Elders at church had just inherited a rather dilapidated, Victorian terraced house in a side street in Leicester, which he sold at basic cost to Mum and Dad. But with limited funds and a short time frame the house needed renovating.

When the church members heard about this, they offered practical and financial help and in the course of two weekends the whole house was rewired, re-plumbed in some places, a new kitchen fitted and the whole house repainted and decorated inside and out. The church predated TV makeover shows by about 40 years. I can remember Mum crying because she was able to choose what colour curtains were put in each room. The whole story could probably fill a book in its own.

This house only had three bedrooms. Ruth got the little one but it wasn't that long before she left to go to college. Mum and Dad had the middle size room. And Alan and I shared the largest room to try and keep two boys nine years different in age as far apart as possible in one room.

Of course I had to change school, and I was sent to Mayflower Junior School. I hated every minute of every day that I spent there. Fortunately for me, I arrived with just one term to go before moving up to secondary school. My teacher was Mister Sage. I thought he was green not wise. He sat me amongst a group of girls and virtually left me to it. The year I was in was streamed as Bright, Average and Thick, I had been put into the average class where all except two were destined for the local secondary modern school. In the Bright class where all except two were heading for grammar school none of them had selected the school I was heading for, so for six months of school and holiday I had no friends. Twice a week the whole school split up into activity clubs, The most popular was the "Ship Club" that did activities around a nautical theme. By this stage I had probably forgotten more about ships than any of the members had learnt. So I was sent to do basket weaving. A soul-destroying activity if "Teacher" insists you just follow the pattern.

At last came the time to move up to the grammar school. I went to the best grammar school and wasted the opportunity (but more of that later). Gateway Boys Technical Grammar School, to give it its full title had only been operating for some 40 years when I started and continued only until the 1980's but in those 60 plus years it set standards and styles that school are still trying to achieve today.

The school day started with the junior forms being lined up and marched round the corner to an almost derelict former congregational church, where school assembly was held; the more senior classes were allowed to make their own way whilst their majesties of the sixth used to gather on the balcony throwing things at the juniors in the stalls below. At the appointed time the Senior Prefects marched in and the staff assembled on the stage and finally the school captain escorted the headmaster to the rostrum. A hymn would be sung and a prayer said then any notices or awards were made all without the headmaster uttering a word. He was Jewish and proud of his heritage but could not by conscience join in Christian worship. He was the first man whose life challenged me about what I believed. We were then marched back to school and to our form rooms. My form master was C W Hardy, proud to be one of only two or three old boys who came back as a teacher, he used to remind us of his time playing rugby for the school when the current school captain was a junior. He was a geography specialist and helped deepen my interest in travel and maps. Then we moved around the school to various classes in different rooms.

I always found homework a trial. I thought then, as I think now, that if the teacher couldn't teach the subject during the lesson time he wasn't much of a teacher. I was always getting into trouble for not doing what was set or forgetting to hand it in for marking, life seemed a perpetual challenge to beat the teacher at not doing homework. The first day I started at Gateway I had to catch the bus from near our house and travel into the city centre then walk through to the school.

Imagine my surprise when I saw another boy heading to the same school in his new uniform, even more when I found out that he lived just around the corner from us less than 100 metres away. Robert (Jammy) James became a casual friend for the next few years. His father ran an undertaker's business and Jammy constantly talked about limousines and polishing the wood of coffins, he couldn't wait to join the family business. Another friend from those days was Dave Elkington, who I recently caught up with again, to find out that he had gone into the Church of England and was a Dean in Newcastle.

Next door to us in Ashover Road sharing the common passageway to the back yards, lived the Parrs. He was the pastor of a congregational church on Humberstone Road and used to ride his bike to all the meetings except Sunday when all the family were lined up and went and caught a bus. There were two children, Susan and Andrew. Susan was a little younger than me, and in the class below me at school. I never stepped inside the next-door neighbour's house. I don't think they knew the bits of the Bible about showing hospitality. But we children used to play together. A favourite game of Susan was persuading her brother to tie her and I up and us having to do forfeits to be released, who knows what that might have led to if we hadn't been caught by my mother coming home from work and looking for me in the garden shed.

Yes, that was another difference because of the reduced circumstance that the family found itself in Mother had had to take a job to help pay the bills, she also took to keeping home accounts of every penny spent on anything. This meant that I often got home and there would be nobody in the house. It was only a short period of my life, and I was old enough to look after myself but it gave me a great sympathy for latch key kids and I decided that if ever I had children, their Mother would be at home for them.

Year two at Gateway and we had a new form teacher, Pickering. I didn't like him, and he didn't like me. On the first day of term, I was elected to be the form captain a position that had some status and privileges. But I, for whatever stupid reason, thought it would be clever to turn down the honour, hoping that I would be persuaded to take it thus enhancing my status even further but Gordon Pickering, on hearing my declamation said, "Good, you weren't good enough for it any way" and immediately appointed the boy who had got second in the ballot. I was still playing at "I don't do homework" at this stage I guess it was about evens in score with the staff.

A few years later a friend took me to meet his hero youth leader from church who had started an Outward Bound centre in the Lake District. Imagine my surprise to find this was Pickering. I think he was as embarrassed as he should have been and could hardly speak to me all day.

Ruth had started at teacher training college, so when Uncle came to visit he moved into the small room. After a few visits around the area, it was decided that he would live with us in the family, but it was obvious that the house was too small. Time to prepare for another move.

If you have an IQ of 100
That means 50% of the population
Are more stupid than you

Chapter 4

KNIGHTON CHURCH ROAD 1963 - 67

As I recounted in a previous chapter when my father was 12 years old, my grandfather died of TB because of the first world war service, and left grandmother with 3 children to bring up in very difficult circumstances. Uncle Harry who had emigrated to Canada agreed to take responsibility for one of the children and so father travelled alone to Canada to a new life. Dad returned to UK in May 1935.

Uncle Harry had also returned to UK in April 1933 and eventually settled in Bristol where he worked as a maintenance man at Wills Cigarettes factory. I remember going on a visit to Bristol to visit my Fathers Uncle, I remember a semi-detached house on the side of a hill with a sweet white haired lady who made a jelly for tea.

Auntie Winnie had now passed away and Uncle came for a visit and stayed with us in Ashover Road. He was a gruff old man who rarely showed his feelings. He smoked a pipe, that stank to high heaven, and I think Mother banished it from the house which left him with the garden shed. He was given the small bedroom which was quite cramped. And with five of us in the house we lived quite close.

How it came about I don't know but Uncle decided to sell up in Bristol and move to Leicester and buy a house jointly with Mum and Dad and move in with us.

I can still remember going to visit potential houses one Saturday afternoon. Mum, Dad and Uncle walked to the first one whilst Alan and I went on our bikes. The first house was OK but we then set off for the second one. The Oldies walked and caught a bus whilst we went ahead on the Bikes. When we saw 77 Knighton Church Road, Alan and I decide this was the one even before the oldies arrived. In due course they arrived and agreed, yes this was the house for us.

It seemed in very short time that Uncle who was retired was renovating 77 and decorating it from top to bottom. As Uncle was doing the work and had paid the lion's share of the money, he chose the colour schemes and the fixtures and fittings. He insisted that the heating was by solid fuel boiler, and to accompany it built the largest fuel bunker any of us had seen. It dominated the view from the kitchen window. After Uncle passed away the heating was converted to Gas and was a lot easier and cleaner to use, the bunker also went, so the family got the patio back. I think Mother particularly had to make many compromises and had to bite her tongue on a regular basis. But in due time we moved in and for a few years had a very happy home there.

Uncle could be quite a gruff character, but sometimes showed his soft centre. On one occasion when I was travelling to school on my bike in icy weather, I managed to fall off the bike and damage it sufficiently that it was un-ride able. I walked home, to find uncle there, Mother was at work, Uncle insisted that I went to school on the bus, even though I would be late. It didn't seem to matter to him that I had hurt my knee, and I felt it was a terrible injustice. The next morning as usual I was late leaving for school, when I remembered my bike was damaged and I would need to catch the bus, this was a problem as I had no money, So I had to ask Uncle to lend me a few shillings. At this point he showed me that he had repaired my bike done a complete maintenance and cleaning job on it, and made it look like new. His comment was "I thought I had better do this or you would have been hanging around the house all day" Gruff old man but a heart of gold.

In due time Uncles health started to decline and very quickly he passed away due to a cancer.

Ever since I could remember we had shown hospitality to people who were visiting the area and attending our church and we regularly had a few students from the university at the church and quite frequently they would come visit the family home for a meal. Some kept coming and other visited only once or twice, Some the family lost contact with, but others are family friends to this day.

At about this time Mother started to take in Lodgers to help fill the family coffers, mostly these were people looking for a few months of accommodation or even for the duration of a university year and most were contacts through the local church we attended. So along with the students there always seemed to be people in the house.

Sunday lunch was the highpoint of the week, As long as I can remember, we always seemed to either have someone visit us or we went to someone else's house, after we moved to 77 we regularly used to entertain students for Sunday lunch, initially these were students who had a background in the brethren movement, who attend our church, but as the years went by all were welcome who were invited by existing attenders, this meant we started to get larger numbers and from differing denominations and backgrounds. How Father paid for it all and Mother prepared it all I can hardly imagine, but there always seemed to be enough but rarely any left over. On one occasion just as he was carving the meat, Father dropped the Pyrex platter, the glass shattered into the meat making the whole lot unusable, surprisingly two tins of corned beef tasted remarkably good with Yorkshire pudding and two veg. As the numbers increased the demand for seats started to outstrip the number of chairs available and all sorts of things were used to make seating including on one occasion a builders plank balanced on blocks, On one occasion we counted that there were 15+ people sitting to have Sunday lunch, including a former president of the Christian Union at Leicester University, the current holder of that post and the elected person for the next year.

Many students went on to significant positions in their careers, and many became leaders in their churches, some became missionaries and I know of one who became a bishop. But one got the highest accolade of all the students we entertained, when she joined the family by marrying my brother Alan,

In one respect it was great to be brought up in this sort of environment, where intelligent people from a variety of backgrounds discussed a range of subjects. Even so I found it very restrictive and couldn't wait to grow up and leave home,

Third year at Gateway was the start of your exam courses after 2 years of general education. My form master was J P White who made an interesting prediction about my future. He forecast that I would either rise to the top of my profession or become a successful criminal. He said I ..." was intelligent enough to achieve anything I wanted but lazy enough to choose the easy option". At the start of the school year we were given tests by many teachers "so they could see where we had got to..." I managed to accumulate 5 marks out of a possible 220 in French and was immediately dropped from the French classes, and because I had a reputation for being "difficult" when a course was oversubscribed, I was one of the ones rejected, so had to take courses that no one wanted.

I was put in the class to do applied Maths with the school deputy head taking the course, Ernie Enderby, had a fearsome reputation as a disciplinarian and we were in real fear of him. He started the first lesson by describing a scenario where two jet fighters are approaching each other at different speeds, altitudes and angles and then asked at what point in time should one pilot fire his missiles to hit the other aircraft. Of course we had no idea, but he said he knew we couldn't work it out yet but that by the end of the year we would be able. Our interest whetted he set about teaching us applied maths with real illustrations. At the end of year exams one of the questions was the problem set in our first lesson, every boy in the class got 100 percent for the exam. The school didn't accept the result and made us resit and, on this occasion, the average mark for all boys was 98%, Not bad for a class of rejects, yes we had learnt how to do the calculations. Ernie was one of the best teachers I ever met, and I am sad to say that I heard he had died alone, with few friends, after his retirement to the Lake District.

Another key teacher for me in those days was Mr A T White. He was a sculptor and also taught pottery and crafts. He wanted people to succeed at something and made sure that they did. I still have some items I made whilst in his classes.

I didn't seem to be very long before we heard that my maternal grandfather, was very ill, He was a severe man, and we learned to behave when we visited their house. We had to sit on a most uncomfortable sofa, and it was definitely speak when you are spoken to. As children we noticed a number of unusual, to us, things some that still amaze me today.

Grandma used to stand the loaf of bread on end, then butter the end and then using the bread knife take a slice horizontally, this left the slice lying on top of the loaf which she then scooped up with the knife blade and deposited it on your side plate. Coffee was never real coffee but "Camp" chicory substitute. Custard was served in a bowl, not a jug. And on Sunday tea, tinned fruit was always served with a slice of bread and butter. They also had a silver miniature carpet sweeper used for sweeping up the crumbs off the tablecloth, the best-behaved child who had eaten all their tea was allowed to use the sweeper, what a treat!!

All the grandchildren were summoned and had to visit grandfather in bed. I remember being more interested in looking round the room, It was the second reception room, because I had never been in there before, than being concerned about grandfather. I realise now that I never went upstairs in that house, in 14 years of visiting.

Then at the weekend I was left alone for most of the time as my parents waited at the bedside, until Grandfather died. During this period, I had to prepare my own meals and discovered that fish finger sandwiches are better with salad cream than Tomato Ketchup or HP sauce. That one strains tinned peas but not baked beans. It seems appropriate that, that knowledge is more significant than the death of my grandfather.

Then after the death of my grandfather, grandmother came to live with us. It had been decided that she was too frail to live alone so she would spend some time with us and then move round the other aunts and uncles. I think it was eleven years later before she moved out to a nursing home for care. Because of her ill health our dining room was converted into a bed sit which curtailed a lot of the pleasure of the house. She still had to go up and down the stairs for the bathroom so I don't see why, to this day, she wasn't given the spare room, and come down for meals, that would have been better for everyone.

During this period as well as mixing with young students our church had quite a good Sunday afternoon Bible study and a weeknight youth activity, I was totally involved in all that was going on. Our youth leader in the early days was Mr John Newton, He was also my cousin by marriage, Kathleen was Uncle Jacks youngest daughter. John systematically taught us the truths of scripture and I still imagine him talking as I remember the lessons we learnt.

Along with all the other things I asked to be baptised as a believer at age 14, I know it was for real but at that age in the family I was brought up in I had no idea about real life. Very soon afterward I was starting to get annoyed with the restrictions of the Brethren and also the restrictions at home. I was ripe for rebellion but didn't know how.

I have vivid memories of being behind with homework. I always hated homework and was regularly in trouble of one form or another for not doing or completing set work. I had an opportunity to catch up but decided that I would rather not bother. That particular weekend I remember going to the Sunday evening service at church and committing myself to serving God if he got me out of trouble. Monday morning and in in school assembly I was called out to attend the second Masters office. Straight on to report and in trouble again. I can still visualise standing in the corridor blaming God for putting me in that position. Three days later it was all due to come out and I funked it. I ran away. I took a jumper with me instead of my schoolbooks in my satchel and ten shillings out of my Post office bank book and hitch hiked to Leeds.

I went to the YMCA and booked a bed in a dormitory for the night and went to the cinema to watch "Carry on Cowboy". Fish and chips for tea and to bed for the night. Next morning I tried to get a job and then realised that my plans were not too realistic. So I hitched a lift to Manchester. Walking round Manchester Piccadilly late on a Friday night was quite eye opening for a young teenager from a sheltered background. Eventually, cold and hungry I went to the local police station to hand myself in. I intended to make it difficult so that they wouldn't know where to send me back to, but the sergeant looked at me sternly and said "name?" and I told him. An hour or so later I was on a train back to Leicester in the care of the train guard.

Money was always tight and as I look back I realise that mum and dad must have made significant sacrifice to give as much as they did. I used to be given 10 shillings each Monday. (50p) in decimal currency. 5 shillings was for school dinners at 1/- per day (5p). 2/6d (12.5p) was for bus fares to get to school 3d each way which left me with 2/6 a week spending money. I soon realised that walking to school or riding my bike doubled my spending money, but even in those days 5 shillings a week was not a lot. So I got a newspaper round, initially just delivering evening papers for which I got paid the princely sum of 7/6 (27.5p) per week, I used to deliver to approximately 75 houses and started in December. After a few days I started knocking on the doors of the houses and offering the "compliments of the season" which elicited a "Christmas Box" usually cash and by the time I had visited most houses I had accumulated nearly £20, I found out some time later that this was equal to at least a week's wages for my father. I then started to do morning papers as well and by the time I stopped working for the news agent I was getting £3.00 a week about 2 days wages for a working man. When I subsequently joined the Royal Navy I was earning £3.50 a week plus food and accommodation.

I was still struggling with school, especially homework, and Girls had appeared like heavenly angels. I think I worked my way, in a platonic way, round most of the eligible girls in our fellowship and several others during the next few years. Several girls stuck in my memory from this period. Bev Bilson, Hilary Heaps, Sue Middlemiss, Liz Giles and Ros Crawley.

The restrictions on a 15/16 year old in a brethren home now became even worse with having to be polite all the time and put up with the mannerisms of elderly relatives. I no longer felt I could invite my friends' round or make any noise etc. It was getting to a point that I wanted out.

I decided to run away again. I did a little more planning on this occasion taking some more clothing and also a larger amount of money. As one always hears about runaways heading for London I went the other way. I headed for Edinburgh. I really had no idea what I intended to do but realising that I was not going to get a job or find anywhere to live I decided to just travel so headed for Bristol. I managed to get to Hawick in the borders before it got dark so slept in a field overnight. It was cold. I hitched on next day until I found a sleeping place near Gloucester. The next day I managed to get to London by noon and then started walking out to get to the M1 It was so hot and I had run out of money I don't think I have ever been so thirsty. I managed to get a drink from a shop and then a lift to Coventry. And eventually made it home.

Of course I was in trouble and when I got back to school they referred me to the Schools Psychological Service. I met with a psychologist several times and then he suggested that I should go to a residential home for kids with psychological problems. I went (no choice) and hated it. It was virtually a prison for kids, most of whom had nothing wrong with them except being kids. I left after a few months no better nor any worse than I had been when I went in.

After I got back home I went to Birmingham to visit what was called the boys and girls exhibition. It was in reality a careers showcase for companies wanting to recruit school leavers. As I had an interest in all things naval I duly visited the Royal Navy stand. Here they were running a competition to name and identify 6 port cities of the world in the shortest time. One had to select six cards from a tub, put them on a grid, identify on a huge world map where they were and flick a numbered switch to illuminate the number at the location. Most kids were taking 2 or 3 minutes to complete this and the fastest to date was about 1 min 30 secs. I stood and observed the situation for a few minutes and realised what the problems were. Many of the kids were not identifying correctly all six places, and the cards were then being thrown into the tub and the next kid picking from the top was getting the same places. After the cards were stood on the grid, the supervisor asked if you were ready and started the stopwatch, the kids then thought about their answer and flicked the switch and so on. So when it came to my turn, I dipped to the bottom of the tub and selected six cards, fortunately I knew all the places and was pretty confident I knew where they were, so I put the cards on the Grid, "Are You Ready?" "No" as I started to memorise the numbers of the switches I needed to use, when I remembered the numbers, I said "Yes, ready" and he said "start" I flicked all six switches and called stop at which he couldn't believe I had done it in 10 seconds. He went and called a supervisor who asked me to repeat the procedure. I picked out the same six cards and did it in 9.5 seconds and won a prize of three days with the navy in a submarine. That summer I travelled with the next two prize winners to Portsmouth, stayed in Barracks overnight, visited ships and the Navy Museum and the Victory then joined HMS Talent for a trip to Weymouth including a submerged section, where we were able steer, etc.

This convinced me that I should join the Royal Navy. I knew my father would not allow me to leave home without opportunity to develop my potential so I could not just join up as a sailor. I had to show I was at least getting a good apprenticeship. Dad took me to a number of factory open days where companies were recruiting school leavers as apprentices but to me the real attraction was that I would be leaving home so none of these really stood a chance. I also found out that to join the navy I had to have passed 5 GCE O levels at grade C or above including Maths, Physics and English. Or I could take the Royal Navy Entrance exam. If I passed that and was accepted after a three day interview board, I could defer my entry to take my GCE's which seemed like a good safety net, to try again if I failed the first one.

Employment for school leavers was not a big problem in those days and in reality, it was a case of choosing which company one wanted to work for. Dad spent a lot of time taking me to various company open days to look at their apprentice schools and I got verbal offers from several eminent engineering companies, but the problem was I would still be living at home and potentially for four to six years, or more.

I was still set on the Navy so in due time the school arranged for me to take the exams spread over a whole day. A few weeks later I was summoned to the headmaster who congratulated me on passing as the 10th highest mark in the country out of 2,000 applicants. Shortly afterwards was invited to Portsmouth for the board which I seemed pass without any problem. I deferred my entry until after I took my GCE's in the summer. Having been expected to take 8 or 9 exams I lost all interest in school, spent more time playing hooky and effectively failed most of my mock exams. I eventually persuaded the school to enter me for 5 GCE's and I was expected to pass 2, Geography and Combined Science, At the end of the day I only managed to pass English Language. But who cared I had my career established already, hadn't I.

Chapter 5

HMS FISGARD 1967 - 68

Although it was a quiet news day for the world media, September 11th 1967, was a most significant Monday, I was joining the Royal Navy. I hardly slept the night before and spent the time packing ready for the off, Breakfast and out the door to catch the bus to the station, Dad had delayed going into work to come and see me off. On the platform he gave me a tiny New Testament and asked me to take it with me everywhere. Dad highlighted 2 verses in Philippians, ch 3 v's 13 & 14. Dad wanted me to have the joy of the life he had experienced, and these verses emphasised an aspect of that. A fresh start and pressing on. I still have it 57 years later.

I met another fellow on the first train who was also going to be an Artificer Apprentice. We changed train at Birmingham for Plymouth and by the time we got there at about 3.00 pm, there must have been 100 others who were joining up the same day. At Plymouth station the Navy collected us up and put us into the back of lorries to transport us to Torpoint and HMS Fisgard.

Artificers have been the technicians of Naval engineering for over 100 years, so we were joining an elite group. The navy wanted us to be happy, so first of all introduced us to Pussers "tea and stickies" that is stewed tea from an urn and a sweet bun with icing on top. Having fed and watered us they led us back to a lecture room where we were told what our commitment to the Navy would be, that we would be subject to Naval Law and we had up to 12 weeks to decide if we liked it or not, so we signed on the dotted line and committed ourselves for twelve years' service after the age of 18. In my case that was a total of 13 years I was signing away even though I was not old enough to vote.

We were then taken to the Naval stores, where we were issued with bedding and taken to our barrack hut, I was in Bennett 1 which held 20 apprentices. About half of this number were from our entry S61, there were 2 or 3 from the entry before ours S60, and 6 or 7 from S59. One of this class was the PO App of the block responsible for discipline, cleaning etc, from S60 there was a Leading App who was delegated most of the responsibility for cleaning. These guys were like school prefects but had all the support of the naval discipline system. In some cases it lead to institutional bullying. But generally these were the good guys.

In my hut that first night I met a fellow called Dave Lee, he had failed his exams and was held back whilst the Navy decided what to do with him. A few days later he was discharged "Services No Longer Required" and sent home. Our divisional Instructor spent a whole session telling us that if we didn't work hard we also would be on the scrap heap like LEE. Not long afterwards we heard that Lee had reinvented himself as a very successful DJ on Pirate Radio and quite often in those early days when playing of songs were often dedicated to someone, he would dedicate a song to "The Tiffys at Fisgard"

For our first week we still wore civvy clothing until we had collected, and marked with our names, all our uniform clothing, everything had a special way of marking it some was just stamped with your name, others you stamped a ribbon and sewed that to the item and some you actually had to embroider the letters as well. I wished my name was Hunt or Hill like two of my colleagues rather than Hodkinson. Then came the day when we felt we blended in when we were able to wear uniform, without caps.

We were not allowed to leave the camp for the first four weeks until we were fit to be seen in uniform on the streets of Plymouth and were not allowed to wear Caps until we had "passed in" to the Navy. To keep us occupied we had to take part in sporting activities. On the first Saturday the PT staff held trials for the various ships teams and as I had played rugby at school I put that as my sport. After ten minutes I realised, as I was taken off for my own safety, that this was man's standard rugby, not school boy level. I was so bad that I couldn't even get a position in our divisional team which left me with the option of Cross Country or Hockey as a sport. I tried CC and after a cold, wet and miserable hour running round fields asked if I could try Hockey even though I had never played before. I was taught the basics of the game over the next few weeks and started to play for the division and was even selected to play for the ship before the Christmas leave. A year later I was awarded my colours for playing Hockey for the ship and enjoyed playing for the next few years even being selected for the Navy on one occasion.

After the first four weeks we "passed in" and were allowed freedom as far as the navy allowed at that time. Every 8 days we were "duty party" and responsible for a variety of tasks, mostly cleaning but also security and safety. Apart from that we had regular work and naval training. We spent about 40% of the time in classrooms doing Maths, English, Science and Technical drawing. 40% in the workshops as previously described and 20% what was called general naval training. This included parade ground drill, sailing, tying knots, adventure training, and everything else to do with being in the Navy including sport. Saturday morning was always Captains inspection of the accommodation followed by "Divisions" which was a parade of the whole camp including an inspection of our No1 uniforms and polished boots.

After new entry training, we were started into class one and basic engineering training, in class one and two we did a few weeks or even a few days of many different trades and departments. This was to give us a general understanding of engineering and to help in deciding which specialisations we were to be trained in. Many hours were spent with a bastard file trying to make a rough irregular piece of steel into a precise dimension squared off block. We also found the time used to sit heavy during the mornings and the afternoons so would regularly ask to be excused to use the heads, and steal a sneaky smoke whilst there. On one occasion the Chief Stoker who was the workshop regulator arrested 20 fellows all hanging around when they should have been working. One other way of getting a sit down in the workshops was to ask permission to go get a haircut, The barbers shop was next to the Chief Stoker's office and when the barber had no business he would wander next door and let it be known he had nothing to do and the Chief would then walk round the workshop and find a victim to be sent for a haircut with a phrase like "Am I causing you pain?" "No, Sir" would be the reply. "Well, I should be, your hair is so long I'm standing on it. Go and get your haircut"

One day working in the heat of the foundry on a hot day I managed to fall asleep at the back of a demonstration. When the instructor noticed he told the class NOT to wake me up but wait until he had finished when he would get me to do the job without benefit of the demo. When I was woken, I was told to get on with it, which I did. I managed to make the complete component and get top marks. When he questioned me about it, I had to admit that I had done more complicated jobs in the school foundry and also when working in a foundry as a casual worker on a couple of occasions. Thank you Gateway I did learn something.

Even our free time was limited. We were allowed leave on Saturday afternoon and Evening until 23.00 hrs, Sunday from 09.00 to 22.00 hrs and Wednesday evening from 18.00 to 21.00 hrs. When we graduated to 2 Class there was the addition of Thursday evening and then in 3 Class Tuesday evening as well. Most of us rarely went ashore during the week except possibly to use the laundrette in nearby Torpoint. We used to get paid every two weeks on a Thursday lunchtime, a portion of our money was held back to pay for laundry, breakages and other incidentals and the balance returned to us on the last pay day before long leave. This of course meant that our limited money rarely spread over two weeks so it was known as pay weekend and blank weekend.

During blank weekend often the exuberance of the apps would turn to pranks of one kind or another. I remember when someone who was tired went to bed early, that the rest of the mess would wait until they were well asleep and then change the clock to 6.30 and wake the slumbering app whilst making out that they were all getting up. With a "wakey, wakey you're late for breakfast" at which the victim would leap out of bed, dress and hurry off out the mess heading for the dining hall, only to find it locked and then to realise it was only 9.30 at night. This worked best in the winter months as it was still dark at both ends of the day. Said victim then had to return to the catcalls of the mess.

For some reason 4 of us decided to go to the cinema in Plymouth one Wednesday night probably to see the new James Bond movie. At some point we suddenly realised that it was 2030 and we had just half an hour to get back. We raced out of the cinema and jumped into a taxi outside and paid him handsomely to get to the ferry as quick as possible. As he pulled up the Ferry was just starting to pull away. The first fellow jumped and made it. Number 2 jumped and landed short in the river, number 3 and I skidded to a halt and pulled out number 2. We had to wait half an hour for the next ferry and by the time we got back to HMS Fisgard we were 58 minutes late. The next day we were put on a charge in front of the commander and fined one day's pay and given two days stoppage of leave. A very expensive missing of the ferry by about 2 minutes. I have been intolerant of bad time keeping ever since.

One thing the Navy loves to do is take trainees out of camp and pretend they are soldiers in the field. In 2 class we went to a base camp on Bodmin moor called Cardinham which was an old China clay pit. We camped out and cooked our own ration packs in February. It was cold and wet and miserable. Here we did abseiling and shooting and most terrifyingly a death slide from top of one of the spoil heaps and out over the flooded pit to the other side. I don't think anyone wanted to do it, but everyone felt elated when it was completed. For a few moments one glowed with warmth.

During the first two terms in Fisgard we were taken on Branch acquaint visits to ships and establishments to find out what the different departments actually did in reality. So we visited RNAS Culdrose to find out about FAA, we also went to RNEC Mandon, HMS Cambridge, HMS Glamorgan. I don't remember any of the visits except that they were what we called "a Jolly" with the exception of HMS Glamorgan, where the shipwright officer was showing us round when a ventilation fan stopped. He nearly freaked out on the spot and dashed off to find out what was happening. When he came back, he ranted on about the skipper getting on at him because so many motors were stopping. I thought he was on the edge of a breakdown. I subsequently found in my career that in most ships the fan motors were not the responsibility of the shipwrights. We were also taken to see the launch of HMS Scylla in Devonport dockyard. She was the last ship built in a Naval dockyard for the Navy.

Towards the end of class two we were able to choose which branch we would be trained in for the future. Each branch had their career path which decided where we would go for part two training. I was not interested in going down the electrical routes and I also knew I wouldn't get selected for Aircraft as they were only looking for 5 out of 250. They told us that we were unlikely to get the choice that we did not want, but they couldn't guarantee even second place. So I chose Aircraft, as first choice, Shipwright as second, Electrical as third and said I did not want Engine Room. I was thrilled to be chosen to be a Shipwright Apprentice.

At this point Shipwrights started doing different workshop activities from the remainder, concentrating on sheet metal work, welding and so on. In our area of the workshop was a sub department, run by a civilian instructor, otherwise known as a Gobby, Mr Draddy. Daddy Draddy as we called him had part of his ear missing, according to legend it had been eaten by a rat when he was a prisoner of war. He constantly walked round with a cigarette in his mouth, he never seemed to tap the ash off until the very end and then lit his next cigarette from the stub of the first. His party piece was to get a billet of steel red hot in the forge and then take it to a saw machine where he gathered the class around him. He then pulled a rope which activated the saw and the class scattered to the four corners of the workshop as it erupted in sparks totally enveloping Daddy Draddy, who reappeared as the process finished with various parts of his overall coat smouldering where the sparks had landed.

As we came to the end of the first year, my natural tendencies came to the fore and I stopped doing homework and took an attitude that I could manage without working, and so I failed my end of year exams. As I only just failed the Navy were kind to me and gave me a second chance by back classing me to S62 entry, 12 of us from all four divisions formed a special class. We carried a reputation and got up to lots of pranks.

In November 1968 I was on duty on a Sunday morning. We got a Tannoy message to report at the

Parade ground "at the rush". This was slang for get there as quick as possible as something serious had happened. When we arrived, the duty Chief ordered us to get into No 1 uniform with gaiters and belts, and report at the Armoury "at the rush" We all dashed off and changed into our best uniforms and boots and reported at the armoury where we were issued with a rifle and bayonet. By this time a bus had arrived, and we were all herded onto the bus which raced out of the camp and down to Torpoint. The rumours of what was happening were getting surreal, from a military coup to alien invaders. On the way we were advised that we were the ceremonial Guard for the Remembrance Day parade. We arrived with minutes to spare and managed a creditable performance. Afterwards some of us were invited for sherry with the mayor. It transpired that the agreement had been made months before, that we would provide the guard and then everyone forgot about it. It was only when the town clerk phoned up to find out where we were that the arrangements were made. It took just 35 minutes to get 30 men on parade in the town 2 miles from the camp. A most unusual duty day.

The time came for passing out exams, on this occasion I did do some work and managed to get top marks but because I was back classed I was not allowed to get recognition for it, so had the highest marks with no prize. The only thing I did get was award of colours for playing Hockey for the ship, but even then, I was given the wrong badge a red one instead of a gold one.. I think this was the only award I ever got for sport.

I then went home for Christmas leave and was drafted to HMS Caledonia in Rosyth, Scotland.

Anecdote

We all had to read daily orders every day for the next day. One thing we had to note was the "Rig of the Day" otherwise known as the uniform appropriate for the activities of that day. Each uniform style was itemised in regulations and we were supposed to conform. During my last term at Fisgard our class was sent across the road to the neighbouring RN establishment where most RN New entry's joined up, for X-ray tests. This place was run by the book or very pusser. As we went in by the main gate, we saluted as was the procedure and were then stopped by the staff on the gate, as the duty officer had decided we were all too scruffy. He inspected us and found out that from the twelve of us, no two were dressed the same, hardly uniform. His punishment to us was to send us to run around the parade ground, well we started going round the outside and gradually cut the corners and took a shorter line until we were walking one behind the other in a circle in the middle. He came and shouted at us until he was literally blue in the face but couldn't take it any further because he had taken it on to himself to punish us and we had to get back to our classes, which was outside of his control, I learned not to give orders that wouldn't or couldn't be obeyed.

"If you write the problem down clearly, then the matter is half solved."

Kidlins Law

Chapter 6

HMS CALEDONIA 1969 - 71

January 1969 saw me travelling up to Scotland to join HMS Caledonia as a 4 class Shpt/App. In some respects, this was the start of the grown up Navy. Even so it was very much like a boarding school. 4 class had to join before 10pm on the Friday night. We were met by a New Zealander PO App, almost a god in his own right, who showed us where to draw bedding and where our beds were, and most importantly where the mess hall was. I was in Benbow division. I managed to incur the wrath of this PO App by asking him which part of Australia he came from. We were in four-man cabins or in some cases, three to a four-man cabin.

Saturday morning saw us all doing joining routine, being issued with drawing instruments, slide rules, coloured pencils and other accoutrements of wonder, then in a typical naval fashion we were allowed leave until Monday morning.

The following weekend we all went on an Exped. Exped or Expedition was the navy's term for Outward bound. It varied in degree and length and intensity but general consisted of being taken to a point and walking over hills calling at several peaks before arriving at the end point where lorries or buses took you back to camp. The 4 class exped was to the Ochils. On the Saturday afternoon we were taken to a field in Glen

Devon where we set up camp. In the evening we walked about a mile or so to the nearest pub, where we drank too much before making our haphazard way back to the camp. Remembering that this is January in Scotland we were not surprised that it snowed overnight. When we set off the next morning to walk over the hills, it was not long before one of our patrol of four, an apprentice from Nigeria decided that he could not go on. There was nothing for it but for the remaining three to assist him and carry his kit as well as our own for the rest of the day. Coming down off the hills into Mill Street, Tillicoultry and seeing the transport waiting was a great relief. Interestingly enough I never revisited Tillicoultry again until 2017 when we moved there to live.

In Cally the procedure was very similar to Fisgard with similar proportions of time spent in the classrooms and workshops as before. We as shipwrights concentrated on our trade training and used to claim that we were "skilled" in many different crafts. I particularly enjoyed the boat repair work and woodwork in general and was fascinated by the little locksmithing that we did. My biggest dislike was arc welding, as I really couldn't see properly the work using the masks provided.

Our Gobby instructor for boat work was not a fan of the new Shipwright officer in charge of our unit. One day he returned from lunch acting as though he had had too much to drink, the officer saw this from his office and came out to investigate. Gobby Dyer then called the class around in a slurred voice and said he was going to demonstrate a Scarfe joint. The officer stood to observe the demonstration, Gobby Dyer then took a plank of timber threw it down on the polished parquet floor, put one foot on the plank to stop it moving and with an adze cut a perfect square feather edge joint without touching the polished floor. When he picked it up and showed the class he just said in a clear sober voice "When you can do that, you will be a shipwright my boys" at which point the officer left.

As shipwrights we were taken onto the Harbour training ships to get some experience in a ship, so we spent a week on HMS Rapid, day running up and down the Forth. After 3 years in the navy I had spent 5 days and no nights at sea.

Like all naval bases everyone had to do a certain number of duties on top of their day work tasks. These normally involved helping with security, cleaning, emergency fire party, cleaning, pulling the flag up, cleaning, pulling the flag down and cleaning. The ships company would be divided into watches and parts of watches that did the duties. In Cally it meant that every 8 days you had to stay on board and do some cleaning. As junior apprentices it tended to pretty menial and at times disgusting so one made every effort to avoid general duties. There were a few special duties and I managed to get into one of those as a "Loch Fitty watch keeper" Back in those days when it seemed that the navy had loads of money. HMS Caledonia had a sailing club based at Loch Fitty 5 or 6 miles from the camp to the Northeast of Dunfermline. Monday to Friday during the day a civvy caretaker looked after the place and kept it clean etc. But from 1800 to 0700 the next morning 2 apprentices were responsible and slept overnight in the club house. We were taken to and from in a pussers tilly. At weekends we went out after lunch on Saturday and stayed until Monday morning. Ostensibly our duties were to assist sailing club members in rigging and launching the boats and providing safety boat cover whilst boats were out sailing. We were supposed to ensure that the premises were secure and only used by naval personnel. Many a happy hour was spent in the local village hostelry, which is now the Half Way Hotel, and many a time the local lasses kept us company during the long evenings, and sometimes longer. I think there were at least two watch keepers who married girls from Kingseat. In the two years I did that duty I can count on the fingers of one hand when we had people out sailing,

Whilst at Fisgard with limited time off starting or developing relationships with girls from back home was quite difficult, but at Caledonia with increased income and more control of our "free time" it was much easier. When I was back in Leicester I used to continue to go to the churches where the girls were and had several longer and more intense friendships. Back in Rosyth I remember meeting a girl at church who invited me back to her parents' home for supper one Sunday evening and offered to cook chips for us, Unfortunately she didn't take the frozen chips out of the plastic bag before putting them in the fryer, plastic caught fire, fire in the kitchen which we managed to put out just before parents returned home, end of potential relationship.

Once a year the Caledonia Amateur Theatrical Society (CATS) put on a production for apps to attend (proceeds for charity) The first year I got involved as Assistant to the stage manager. The second year I actual had a leading role in the play. I was not really a good thespian, but it did provide some light relief.

Alan and some of the other young folk from the church in Leicester used to travel to Lowestoft for the East Anglia young people house party every Easter . This was a conference organised by a committee of folk from the churches in East Anglia which had several functions, a wholesome holiday weekend, Bible teaching to encourage young Christians, A time to promote and excite young Christians about missionary service and, it was a venue to meet suitable young people of the opposite sex. I had been with Alan on several occasions, and at one of them met a young lady called Chris Turley. We developed a friendship and I used to travel from Rosyth to Hertford for a weekend to spend time with her at her college. I had more money than sense.

Whilst in Cally I was involved with sailing and occasionally would crew a sea going yacht to the various regattas up and down the Firth of Forth, We would generally sail out on Saturday afternoon, anchor at the local port and then race on Sunday morning and back to Rosyth Sunday afternoon, The skipper was generally an officer from somewhere in the base and not necessarily from Cally, so they used to treat us like adults rather than delinquent school boys.

One of these officers announced that he was putting together a crew to bring an MFV back to Rosyth and would we be interested in being part of it. As it would be a break from routine I said "Yes". In due time he got permission, and it was approved that I could go. I think there were two other apps going as well. We met together and were taken to Inverkeithing station on a Thursday evening. There was apart from the two ringer a PO, a Leading Seaman, two other seaman and the three apps. At this point we had no idea where we were going. Train to Perth and on to Inverness arriving about midnight, Train due to leave Inverness for Thurso at 4.00 am so we snuck on board and got our heads down, Morning found us arriving in Thurso and then on to Scrabster, We purchased provisions on the way at the local supermarket £30.00 for food and £70.00 for drink.

Arriving in Scrabster we waited for a 75 ft MFV which discharged a group of divers. We then took over and sailed out into the Pentland Firth some of the roughest waters around the UK and on to Aberdeen. It was the first time I stood night watches on the wheel, just a leading hand and myself. Fortunately, the officer in charge was sleeping in his cabin behind the bridge and if we had any problems, we just opened the wheelhouse window and banged on the roof. We arrived in Aberdeen mid-afternoon and slept for a few hours before heading for the town for a Saturday night. Sunday morning, with a heavy head, we set sail for Rosyth. For some reason it seemed to take for ever and we arrived about 4.00 am Monday morning. I was due on a ceremonial parade for the passing out class at about 9.00 but was surprisingly allowed to miss it and so was able to get away for leave at midday with everyone else. Leave was generally in Leicester and the most interesting parts were meeting up with the various young ladies of the church.

I never really got on well with the studies at Cally. At the end of 6 class, we took annual exams and I managed to get the prize for schoolwork, but this was probably due to having time to study whilst in Sickbay recovering from Glandular fever. I actually missed the exams and had to take them at the resits. Even with this I was never given an apprentice rating, I subsequently found out that I had negative reports written on my records, which were erroneous. My DO should have read these reports to me so I could contest them, but he didn't. This was held against me for the next 3 years of naval service and it was only later at a leadership course that I was shown my record and managed to get the reports removed.

Throughout our apprenticeship with each subject, we did we had to do small tests to show we had learnt each stage, If we achieved over a certain percentage score we were allowed to keep these small tests, I was pleased to keep several and still have one or two.

Every year we had also to pass the Naval Air and Marine Engineering Board (NAMEB) tests before we could proceed to the next stage. The Metal work test I took in 8 class lasted 40 hours. I was more than pleased to finish it and move on. In 10 class we had to do a woodwork test, which again was 40 hours to make a Bedside cabinet with a drawer. I was thrilled to get this to keep and took it home and gave it to my mother. So as not to spoil it she got dad to put a Formica top on it to stop her teacup making rings. At some point he also painted it rather heavily. After Mum moved into the care home when Dad passed away, I liberated the cabinet and managed to restore it. I still have it beside my bed 57 years after I made it.

By the time I got to 9 class I had passed several of my trade tests and schooling was progressing OK. I had managed to get my ONC in Naval Architecture. We were due to travel across Scotland to visit HMS Neptune, at Faslane, the navy's nuclear submarine base. And the day before we were off I got a message from home that my best friend John Allen had died suddenly the previous weekend and that the funeral was on the next day. I asked for and was given compassionate leave, travelled overnight and was able to attend the funeral the next day. John was only 19. I have never had another friend who I could relate with as well as him, I still miss him nearly 57 years later.

Ten class as senior apprentices was mostly spent completing small aspects of our training and preparing and equipping us to go to sea in the real Navy. During this period, we had some chance to state our preference of ship to go to from a list. Those who were CPO apps and PO apps had first choice and then it filtered down. I did not realise that one could find out what the ships future programme was and use that to help select your draft. So I just chose a ship that sounded like it was OK, I didn't know where it was based, where it was going or even what type of ship it was except it was a frigate. But they made good cars so HMS Jaguar must be OK.

The last week at Cally was as hectic as any time in my naval career, All our Kit was inspected, we were issued with tropical uniforms, Medical vaccinations had to be up to date. All documentation and travel documents were issued. We had lectures on living on a ship and practical self-defence training given by Marine sergeants.

We had to do life raft training which comprised jumping off the top diving board, swimming to the life raft container, self-inflating it, as if it had not inflated automatically, turning the right way up if necessary. If it was not necessary the instructor would flip it over so we had to right it. Then we had to climb inside, all 20 of us. I was surprised how much more difficult it was than we had thought it would be.

We had a formal passing out class dinner with the Captain, Senior Officers, Staff instructors and Civilian Instructors as our guests. Our class upset the protocol and invited the mess block cleaners as well. This event was held at the Glen Eagles Hotel and was an event to remember.

Finally, we practiced for the passing out parade. Most fellows had invited their parents and there was a fair sprinkling of senior officers about. The salute and presentation of prizes was by the Flag Officer Scotland and Northern Ireland. Initially I had been a member of the passing out guard but due to numbers involved there was 1 person too many to make equal number of files, so I was relegated to car door opener for the admiral, which suited me fine apart from stepping forward at the correct time and doing the necessary I was out of sight and hopefully out of mind. All went well until the Friday afternoon before the parade when the Captain conducted a dress rehearsal. He wanted to know why I wasn't on the parade and wasn't happy with the gunnery officer's explanation, but it was too late to put me back in the main guard. However on this parade and only on this parade each year there was a special cutlass guard made up of the 6 CPO apps of the camp. He suggested that it would not be out of place to have 7 in a single line guard so that is where I was placed. I had to learn how to do cutlass drill in 2 days before the parade on Monday morning. My parents and sister had arrived for the weekend. Somehow, I managed to fit everything in and the parade went off without a hitch from my point of view.

Because I was due to join a ship overseas. I was to fly out from RAF Brize Norton. This meant that the Navy would ship part of my kit and part of my toolkit to the ship, but I had to carry the balance. I had 2 suitcases weight 40 Kg and a tool kit weight 28 Kg. I also had my bedside cabinet to carry. We loaded some of my kit into the 4th seat of my sister's car and she took it home whilst I travelled home on the train. I was ready for leave and to travel to my new draft.

95% of quoted statistics are made up on the spot.

This rises to 98.5% in bars

Chapter 7

HMS JAGUAR 1971 - 72

I had been in the navy for 3 years and 8 months when I passed out of HMS Caledonia on 19th April 1971 I was 20 years of age and confident of my future. I was looking forward to nearly 3 weeks leave before reporting to RAF Lynham in Wiltshire to fly out to join HMS Jaguar in Gibraltar. Because I was flying out I had returned most of my toolkit except for a "flying Kit" which weighed nearly 25 Kg. Most of my kit was packed in a Kitbag which the navy transported for me and I was allowed 2 suitcases total weight 30 Kg.

However after 10 days leave I returned home one afternoon to find a police car at the house. The police sergeant told me I had been recalled from leave and that I was to report to Portland at 0800 the next morning. This would be impossible using public transport so a visit to the police station was necessary to advise the naval authority that it was impossible and to get me a new travel warrant.

I eventually left from Leicester station at about 10.00pm and arrived at Weymouth at 9.30ish the next morning, I then had to blag a lift to the Naval base at Portland humping all my kit with me. There I reported to an office who told me to be at a jetty near the office at 2.30 pm, I had to hump all my kit up to the nearest naval camp HMS Osprey to get some lunch and then hump it back.

There was still no sign of the ship but a boat appeared and several folk and an officer got on board followed by me and my kit. We motored out into the middle of Portland Harbour, meanwhile HMS Jaguar came into harbour through one of the entrances and we went alongside her. A ladder came down the side and one by one in seniority order, me last, we climbed up whilst someone hauled my kit up on deck. I was greeted by a chief who took my kit and put it in a locker and introduced himself as Shipwright Earl. By this time the ship had passed back out of the harbour entrance and was proceeding at speed somewhere. I was taken to the stokers mess and met Terry Crotty who was a Shipwright 3rd and my senior. He got me a drink of tea in a whiskey glass and explained that we would be at action stations in 10 minutes time. So I then ended up at Action stations in number 1 uniform in the middle of the Thursday war.

On completion of the exercise I went back to the mess and found a bunk and locker and got some food. Jan Snell was the killick of the mess. Jaguar had returned to harbour and secured alongside. Someone then asked me if I was going ashore. I said that apart from making a phone call I intended getting my head down to catch up from travelling all the previous night. Would I mind doing a sub as fire party so someone else could go ashore which I agreed to do. Phone call home to tell mum I had arrived OK and that I would phone to let her know what was happening. and so to bed. Next morning I woke up to find the ship at sea and proceeding to Gibraltar. It was to be 11 months before I made the next call home.

At this point I started my life skills training and some of the best days of my life.

As a "Tiff" we were in a privileged position, due to our technical training we received accelerated promotion, so that although I joined the ship as an apprentice just 8 months later I was going to be promoted to 3rd Class which was equal to a leading hand. This could lead to some enmity where one was in a messdeck with guys who might spend 8 to 10 years as a stoker and when promoted to leading stoker might get no further. There were all kinds of people in the mess. Some were career guys who did climb the ladder for their own betterment. Whilst others were just doing their time and would leave the navy after 10 years at the same rank as they joined. It was a wise "Tiff" who learnt to keep his opinions to himself, and his mouth shut.

HMS Jaguar was one of the first class of ship that was designed and built for the RN after the 2nd World War, so although there were several innovative design features she was also built on some old-world principles, for example we had what was known as "broadside messing" which principle goes back as far as Nelson and beyond.

The messdeck was an area of about 20 ft forward to aft and 40 ft abeam. Into that space some 30 men had bunks, Lockers and wardrobes as well as suitcase stowage. In some messes on the ship fellows were having to sleep in hammocks, Just to make life more interesting there were two large hatches that occupied deck space to give access to a store room and a magazine below our mess. Also running through the mess were the hoists that took shells from the magazine up two decks to the gun turret above. And finally, we had to have two or Three tables and a fridge in the mess as that was where we ate our meals and spent our off watch social time.

It was an interesting experience getting food until one got used to it. We collected a divided tray and climbed the ladder out of the mess then made way forward to where there was a server in the passageway at the Galley then collecting your meal made your way back to the mess, down the ladder and found a place to eat. Each mess was issued with tea coffee and sugar and either fresh or powdered milk according to whether we were alongside or at sea. We were also issued with cups and cutlery on a regular and frequent basis. Someone would put tea in a teapot and go and get boiling water from the tap at the galley so you could get a drink with your meal. Then someone would take a bucket shaped container, known as a fanny, to the galley and get boiling water and a squeeze of washing up liquid. This was to wash the dishes, Put the scraps in a bucket and dip the tray in the fanny swish with a dish mop and it was done. BUT if you dropped the cutlery in the fanny, it was too hot to fish them out so many people just left them. As the meal progressed the water cooled but also acquired a floating scum that often put more dirt on the plates than it took off but also dissuaded one from putting your hands in. The last man took the washing up fanny up to the aft deck of the ship and tipped the water down a gash shute into the sea. If this had an accompanying rattle you learnt that someone had dropped their cutlery, and it was not going to come back. Hence the need for regular issues.

I soon settled into the working routine. We all used to meet in the workshop at the start of the day, Shipwright Bob Earl would give out the tasks and duties for the day. Bob was a good boss prepared to give a little leeway if you were making an effort but would jump all over you if you were swinging the lead. The team initially was Bob, Terry Crotty 3rd and me as an App. We also had two sailors who acted as mates and cleaning party. Our workshop was right forward. Only the paint shop through the collision bulkhead forrad of us. It did mean that one soon learnt to cope with the ups and downs of the ship in any sort of seaway. Alternatively, we found a job somewhere else on the ship that was more comfortable. Every other day I would be "duty shipwright". This meant that should there be any faults or defects in our part of ship we just set to and fixed it. The normal things were AC units breaking down or plumbing blockages and leaks. Should there be more significant problems Bob would also advise and help. We will hear more about some of these later.

First foreign port for Jaguar was Gibraltar. Gib was, at that time, a large naval base with dockyard facilities and everything that went with that. At this time the border with Spain was closed due to political conflict so it was virtually an Island. Having played (Field) hockey at Fisgard and Caledonia I was selected to play for Jaguar, also on the team was the skipper. I learnt that playing hockey on tarmac in the afternoon summer heat was a lot harder, quicker and harder than I was prepared to put up with and I never played hockey again. After just two nights we left and went back out into the Atlantic on our way to Teneriffe.

Teneriffe with a trip up El Teide, then on to Tristan da Cunha, the most remote inhabited Island in the world. A few years previously the volcano that is the island had erupted and all the inhabitants had been evacuated, later they returned and we were the first RN ship to visit since their return and we were checking that everything was OK. Again an opportunity to go up the volcano. And on to Simonstown in the RSA.

Simonstown is the Naval base for the RSA Navy nearest to Cape Town so runs ashore tended to be in Cape Town. This gave the opportunity to go to the top of Table Mountain but I had learnt about going up mountains so this time it was by cable car.

The following section is extracted from the ships log to give a sense of where we went. I will interleave it with some incident stories

Items written in Italics are my comments

Items written in this form are from the log daily summary

Tuesday 11 May '71
    1045   Hands to Harbour stations for departure TENERIFFE

Monday 17 May '71
    2030   Cross the line

Tuesday 18 May '71
Ceremony of Crossing the line cancelled due to unsuitable weather.
Passed Ascension Island

Wednesday 26 May '71
    1524   Anchored TRISTAN da CUNHA
From 24/5/71 to 29/5/71 the ship patrolled around the islands of Tristan and Gough Island.

Wednesday 2 Jun '71
    1145   Mail drop by SAAF, canisters recovered by Gemini

Thursday 3 Jun '71
    0845 – 0930 Procedure Alpha Arrival SIMONSTOWN
Leave until 0900 next day

Wednesday 9 Jun '71
    1000   Depart SIMONSTOWN

Sunday 13 Jun '71
              At BEIRA patrol
0630   Solids RAS – Tarbetness
0900   Alongside RFA Derwentdale – Fuel
1359   Alongside HMS Dido – Heaving line transfer
Films
1818   Make passage to Gan

Sunday 20 Jun '71
0745   Hands to Harbour stations, Arrival GAN
1145   Hands to harbour stations, Depart GAN

Saturday 26 Jun '71
0730   SSD and Cable party
0915   Alongside No1 Stores Basin, Sembewang, SINGAPORE

Leave until 0800

Log entries were few and far between. Patrol/OOG/Ships entering and leaving harbour/official visitors

Monday 19 Jul '71
              Action Departure SINGAPORE
0940   Chaplain joins for passage to Sydney
1045   Hands to Action Stations NBCD 1Z
1105   Slip from Stores Basin – proceed to Sea
1825   Hands to Defence Stations

    Casex *Various exercises whilst in defence watches with HM Ships Danae, Achilles, HMNZS Otago, and RFA's Resource, Tidepool, Tarbetness, and Olna*

Wednesday 4 Aug '71
              Arrive SYDNEY

Enter harbour pass under the bridge, round Cockatoo Island and back
1018   Berth at SW Cruiser Wharf, Garden Island

Monday 9 Aug '71
   0900   Depart SYDNEY

Wednesday 11 Aug '71
   0830   Board and tow RFA Reliant
   1930   Planeguard for HMS Eagle

Thursday 12 Aug '71
               Screen HMS Eagle

Acted as a KOTLIN Class Destroyer, attacked HMS Danae, HMAS Yarra, HMAS Swan, RAS RFA Tideflow

Friday 20 Aug '71
   0900   Arrived DUNEDIN

Thursday 26 Aug '71
   1000   Depart DUNEDIN

Friday 27 Aug '71
               Visit to Milford Sound

Saturday 28 Aug '71
               RV HMS Eagle

Thursday 2 Aug '71
   0900   Arrive ESPERANCE BAY, Berth South Side, Tanker Jetty

Friday 3 Aug '71
   1400 – 1630 Ship open to visitors. 587 attended

Sunday 5 Aug '71
   1000   Depart ESPERANCE

Tuesday 7 Sept '71
   My 21st Birthday, at sea

Thursday 9 Sept '71
    0900   Arrive BUNBURY, berth Land Backed Jetty

During the visit to Bunbury I was invited to visit the home of some friends of my parents, the Siddons, who lived in Perth. The invited the youth group from their church to their home on the Saturday night and threw a 21st birthday party for me. I also got a phone call from my parents during that evening. It was at church with them the next day that I recommitted myself to Christ and this had a subsequent effect on my attitude to military service as a way of life and probably hastened my decision to leave the RN.

Tuesday 14 Sept '71
    0730   Depart BUNBURY

Friday 24 Sept '71
    Secured alongside 6 south berth, SINGAPORE

Friday 8 Oct '71
    0900   Ships company move into HMS Terror
No mention is recorded of when they returned on board. During this time major repairs were carried out on the main engines by the ships company.

Thursday 25 Nov '71
    0905   slipped from jetty

Friday 26 Nov '71
    2030   secured No3 Berth

Saturday 27 Nov '71
    1000   slip and proceed, Depart SINGAPORE

Tuesday 30 Nov '71

At Sea, on way to Hong Kong.
Weather force 9, damage done to FX during day, reduced speed

1 Dec '71 and 2 Dec '71
At Sea, Looking for survivors of SS Great Ocean
Lifeboat found, No Survivors

Friday 3 Dec '71
    1005   Berthed alongside HONG KONG, "West Arm, HMS Tamar"

Thursday 9 Dec '71
    0900   Cdr Hunt Joins
    1205   Cdr Collins left ship

Monday 13 Dec '71
    0900   slipped, Depart HONG KONG

Thursday 16 Dec '71
    1400   Berthed, Alava Ext, SUBIC BAY

Monday 20 Dec '71
    0900   Depart SUBIC BAY

Wednesday 22 Dec '71
    0840   Secure, North Wall, HMS Tamar, HONG KONG

Christmas Day 25 Dec '71
I was on Shore Patrol, including an incident on Jaguar involving AB Patterson

Sunday 26 Dec '71
    0215   App Hodkinson returns on board, patrol

Tuesday 28 Dec '71

    1400   Cold move to Wampoa Drydock

Thursday 30 Dec '71

I was promoted to Shpt 3 (Leading Hand)

Friday 31 Dec '71
    1210   A/B Patterson and escort to BMH
    1220   Ord/Sea Norton and escort to Tamar
    1235   A/B Patterson and escort return to ship
    1330   Ord/Sea Norton's escort return
    1335   A/B Patterson and escort to Stonecutters

One of the joys of being promoted was that I changed duty roster, having done shore patrol as an app on Christmas day, I went on to the leading hand roster, and as the new boy got to do shore patrol on New Year's eve.

Sunday 09 Jan '72

Former Cunard liner SS Queen Elizabeth on Fire in Harbour.

Monday 10 Jan '72
    1300   Depart for Singapore

Thursday 14 Jan '72
    0900   Arrive Singapore, Berth 6 Stbd side to.

Friday 21 Jan '72
0900   Depart Singapore to Gan

Wednesday 26 Jan '72
    0900   Gan. Berthed alongside RFA Wave Ruler

Thursday 27 Jan '72
    22.00   Weighed Anchor. Proceed on Passage to
                    Massawa, Ethiopia

Tuesday 1 Feb '72
At Sea, Stopped Engines to "Paint Ship"

Wednesday 2 Feb '72
11.30 Procedure Alpha,
12.00 Alongside, Pt side to, Massawa

Thursday 3 Feb '72
Make and Mend Leave, from 1230

Friday 4 Feb '72
  "Massawa Navy Days"

Sunday 6 Feb '72
Sea Day
0800 Dress Ship - Accession Day. Proceed to Sea
1550 Alongside

Monday 7 Feb '72
0900 HIM Haile Selassie Arrives on board
 (21 gun salute)
0935 HIM Haile Selassie Leaves
 (21 gun salute)
1020 Slip and proceed, Passage to Mombasa

Saturday 12 Feb '72
0930 Secured Mombasa, K1-K buoys, Killindini

Whilst in Mombasa I took Local overseas leave at "Silversands" camp and also enjoyed a Safari to Tsavo national park and Voi Safari lodge

Thursday 24 Feb '72
0900 Slip proceed to Beira

Sunday 27 Feb '72
2000 Patrolling off Beira

Monday 28 Feb '72
  0912   RAS RFA Orangeleaf
  1820   Mail from Orangeleaf

Monday 6 Mar '72
  am   RAS(L) – RFA Tidereach
  Pm   RAS(S) – RFA Stromness

Monday 13 Mar '72
  Passage to Simonstown

Thursday 16 Mar '72
  1150   Maildrop from SAAF Shackleton

Friday 17 Mar '72
  0900   Simonstown

Wednesday 22 Mar '72
  1350   Citadel Test
  1555   Citadel test complete

Friday 24 Mar '72
  1000   Slip, proceed to Gibraltar

Wednesday 29 Mar '72
  Off St Helena
  Am   RAS RFA Tidereach
  Pm   Boarding Exercise on RFA Tidereach

Friday 31 Mar '72
  Good Friday - Sunday Routine

Saturday 1 Apr '72
  Sunday routine   Hands to Bathe

Sunday 2 Apr '72
  Easter Day - Sunday routine

Friday 7 Apr '72
  1455   Special Sea Dutymen

    1507   Alongside Gibraltar

Monday 10 Apr '72
    0900   Slip proceed UK

Thursday 13 Apr '72
    0700   Anchor – Spithead
    1040   Weighed
    1128   Alongside Portsmouth

I went on leave from Portsmouth and returned to Chatham where the ship then was. This was so that during the month of May the ship could do an Assisted maintenance Period whilst most of the ships company went on leave.

In June on completion of the maintenance period we went to Portsmouth and on to Portland where we did a mini "work up" On the 17th of June we practiced "Ship open to the Public" This coincided with my brother and his family being on holiday in nearby Weymouth. They came to visit and Sharon decided to join the Wrens, but that is another story.

From Portland we went to Minehead This was followed by a visit to Teignmouth and other visits and exercises in the English Channel areas during July rounded off by another maintenance in Chatham during August. At the end of the month, the ship was involved in Navy Days before sailing for Gibraltar on the 29th of August.

September was spent as the Gibraltar Guard ship. After a quick trip to Malta and ended with a 3 day trip to Tangier. In October we again went to Malta where we joined up with STANAVFORMED otherwise known as "NATO Standing Naval Force in the Mediterranean." This was a group of 5 Frigates, One each from UK, USA, Italy, Greece and Turkey. There was a small amount of crew exchange and attempts to work with potential allies should there be a need. First port of Call was Izmir in Turkey. I took the opportunity to visit the ruins at Ephesus, Then on to Kalamata in Greece where we enjoyed some of the best olives in the world. Finally we travelled to Trieste, Italy and I took the opportunity to visit Venice.

We were back in Chatham at the beginning of November to give leave before going to Rosyth to take on Ammunition and leaving there on the 27th to go on Fishery protection patrol around Iceland, otherwise known as the "Cod War" Whilst there we encountered some heavy weather which was to be expected in December in the North Atlantic. We sustained some damage so had to leave again and de-ammunitioned at Crombie pier on 18th of December before proceeding to Chatham arriving late afternoon of 19th.

I was promoted to 2nd Class (PO) on the 20th and went on leave and draft to HMS Hermes on 23rd December.

During my time on Jaguar, I changed from being an overconfident arrogant apprentice to a qualified confident tradesman able to put my training into practice. I had learnt how to live in a junior rates messdeck and not be punched every day. How to take responsibility for some quite large projects.

Anecdote

Jaguar was getting a little long in the tooth and was prone to a number of problems. When we used to do anti-submarine exercises, the squid launcher used to fire the depth charges over the ship toward the submarine and the ship continued to sail in the same direction so was from time to time over the position that the depth charges exploded. This shook the ship violently, which quite often caused leaks to occur where inlet pipes came into the ship. Not huge amounts but a steady trickle. As the chippy party we would be called to isolate the problem and build a concrete box around the area to stop the leak until it could be permanently repaired. We used to carry quick hardening underwater cement for the purpose.

Quite often we would be called out a few hours after the exercise to go to a space and do the repair. For a laugh we used to put our life jackets on whilst walking through the ship to get the materials necessary. On one occasion we were asked by a junior sailor what was going on, so we told him that we were going to repair a leak in the ship bottom to stop us sinking.

The next day the leading hand of the junior's mess asked us to stop wearing lifejackets when we didn't need to as he had had problems the night before stopping the juniors trying to sleep in their hammocks wearing lifejackets.

If you want to give credit for a Quotation

But can't remember who said it

The following are the most popular to use

Cicero

Shakespeare

Mark Twain

Winston Churchill

Chapter 8

HMS HERMES 1973-75

I had enjoyed and loved my time on Jaguar so much that I had taken very little leave, so when I was drafted just before Christmas in December 1972 to get all my leave due in, I had 8 weeks leave and did not join Hermes in Plymouth until the end of February. At the time Hermes was completing a major refit to convert her from being a "fixed Wing" aircraft carrier to a "Commando" Carrier. This meant that the ships company were accommodated in Drake Barracks, Devonport. Whilst the ship was in the dockyard basin.

I arrived on a Thursday and spent most of the afternoon getting accommodation in Drake and doing joining routine. Friday morning I reported to the chippies office and was given a task laying some tiles, I was working alone and didn't know my way round the ship, I missed stand easy but went to the dockside canteen for lunch, Oggie and coffee, On returning to the ship I realised that there were not many folk working. No one had thought to tell me that dockyard routine was to finish at lunch time on a Friday unless you were duty over the weekend.

This was the start of my disillusionment with the Navy. When I selected the specialisation that I chose we were told that there was a 50 / 50 ratio for sea/shore time. Having spent 2 years at sea with Jaguar I was expecting a 2-year shore posting, I was told that Hermes was commissioning in August so would have

8 months shore time. I had already had 2 of those months as leave that was due to me, so it was reduced to 6 months.

Whilst in HMS Drake I was accommodated in the Senior rates mess. It was a 6-story building, On the ground floor were the lounges, bars and TV rooms as well as the dining room. Above that it comprised corridors of single cabins with communal bathrooms. There were no lifts to each level. Unless you happened to meet your neighbours in the corridor one didn't necessarily know who lived next door. Each Senior rates mess set their own rules but were generally of a similar arrangement. One consistent item was that members changed into blue suits or evening wear for dinner and using the bar in the evening. In Drake at that time one was required to wear blue suits for all meals. This meant for those accommodated from ships in the dockyard that they had to do the following procedure. Getup, put on a blue suit, walk down 4 or 5 flights of stairs, get breakfast, go back up 5 flights of stairs change into working rig, go down 5 flights and walk down to the ship in the yard. At lunch time this was repeated, and also again in the evening. Most of us preferred to buy food in the dockyard canteens. I still love Cornish pasties.

One week later I was drafted to HMS Royal Arthur, which was the Navy's Petty Officer Leadership school, for 6 weeks. It was at Royal Arthur that I found out that my divisional officer back in Caledonia had incorrectly and illegally marked my card. It took a lot of effort to get his remarks (that applied to someone else) removed and probably too late.

After 6 weeks I went back to Hermes only to go on Easter leave. Straight after leave the ships company moved on board and with about 200 dockyard mateys also on board we went to sea for sea trials for 4 weeks. I remember a significant event whilst at sea on the trials. One of the systems being tested was the aircraft refuelling system in the hanger. A dockyard worker opened a valve on the system to check it, but a section of pipe had been removed for some purpose and not replaced. He then couldn't turn off the valve so was pumping Aviation Fuel into the hanger. Most of it went into the lift well where it was found that the drains from there overboard were blocked with rubbish and debris.

This meant that the ship became a floating Bomb, one cigarette or a spark could set it off. So the ship went to emergency stations whilst the chippies tried to clear the drains. Eventually all the dockies were persuaded to stop smoking and all non-essential people gathered on the flight deck. After half an hour people were getting restless so the PTI's organised a game of deck hockey about 350 per side and about 5 pucks in play at the same time. Then they organised a tug of war using the towing hawser, this kept every one busy until some of the crew tied their end off , leaving the dockies trying to shorten the ship by pulling the front to the back. It took about 5 hours to stand down and there was a rumour that some dockies put in for overtime because they were not free to "do as they liked", even though they spent most of the time sunbathing on deck.

I was then posted to HMS Phoenix to do the NBCDi course for 6 weeks. Summer leave and back for the ships commissioning. So, in the 8 months of my shore time, I don't think I actually unpacked my suitcase. By the time I moved on board and the ship sailed I was well and truly fed up. Chokka.

In the definitive book about Hermes by Lt Cdr Tony Dyson, the next 18 months are covered in less than one and a half pages. We sailed to do anti-submarine training and then visited Oslo, in Norway, We then took Marines for training in Skye before having Christmas at Devonport. We then sailed to Rosyth to pick up 45 commando. It was here that Hermes managed to snag some old wires with her anchors that took so long to clear that she could no longer get under the bridges. Off to Narvik to deposit the marines for their exercises. This was enlivened by going to search for the British trawler Gaul. This was the worst weather I ever experienced in the North Atlantic and Arctic Oceans. It was recorded as Force 12 on the Beaufort scale with mountainous waves. The ship had the walkways ripped off either side of the flight deck by the sea. Emergency repairs took all weekend once we were back in shelter.

On to Hamburg and then out to the Mediterranean to Malta. While the ship was in Malta the captains launch needed an engine change. I was detailed off to take out the woodwork to facilitate the engineers to remove one engine and replace it with another. When I went back next day to replace the frames and floorboards the chief in charge told me not to complete it until we had done sea trials. So off we went around the coast for a swim. Not surprisingly we needed to test again the next day, and on this occasion we took some beer. After a week we did complete the job and sign off the work. The ship exercised with NATO forces off Cyprus before picking up 41 commando and taking them to St John, New Brunswick. Hermes went to Halifax for self-maintenance before going to Bermuda and New York (on 4th July) and back to St John to pick up 41.

Halfway across the Atlantic on the way to Malta we were advised of the international situation developing in Cyprus between the Greeks and the Turks. Hermes went to full power and leaving all the attendant ships behind we got to Malta in short time. We landed a number of Marines from 41 and picked up others and also picked up a range of stores and ammunition for them. Then continued at full speed to the Akrotiri area of southern Cyprus We landed most of 41 and then we were advised that the Turks had invaded Northern Cyprus at Kyrenia. We headed there with the intention of evacuating British holidaymakers from the area. On the way we prepared for having a thousand or so civvies on board including ladies who needed separate toilets and bathing facilities. In due course we entered the "Turkish War Danger Area" on 23rd July 1974. Along with the other ships with Hermes we rescued 5,171 British holiday makers and 2,350 other people from different nationalities the ship then transited to Akrotiri and transferred people ashore for repatriation, most of the people passed through Hermes at one time or another.

Due to the delay in returning to UK as planned it was decided to send a group of crew home to go on leave so that when the ship returned to UK we could start the maintenance period straight away and get back on schedule. I was detailed off for this group so flew home by "Crab" air due to flight restrictions we had to fly a long way round in propellor powered aircraft that took about 8 hours. It would have been quicker to fly to America.

We did a maintenance period in Devonport before picking up Dutch "Cloggies" for Exercise Northern merger off northern Norway. A Trip to Copenhagen and Cherbourg before converting to ASW and exercises in the North Atlantic during November. Hermes then went to Devonport

I had decided some time earlier to leave the Navy and try something different, so I left in March 1975. I often wonder if things had gone slightly differently if I would have continued and possibly completed time for pension as many of my friends and colleagues did.

Chapter 9

LEAVING THE RN 1975 -79

I arrived home from Plymouth in early 1975. I was in a long-term relationship with Janet Wigney. I had no preparation for life and work in civilian life. I had no savings, no job and no home. I don't think I asked Mum and Dad if I could move in with them but just arrived home. It was less than ideal. I hoped to join the police force and had filled in the papers to join the Leicestershire constabulary.

I was asked to attend their interview day and, as I wore glasses to bring the optical prescription with me. On arrival at the force headquarters, I registered with reception and was relieved of my glasses prescription and sent to a classroom. Shortly afterwards an instructor arrived and sent several guys home because they had not brought with them the items we were instructed to bring. We were told that if you couldn't obey simple instructions, they would not accept you. At this point someone came to the door and called me out and told me that I had failed the minimum standard of eyesight for a policeman so I should go home.

This meant that I now had no plans to get a job as well. I subsequently found out that Leicestershire had the highest standard of all UK police forces at that time, and that I could have walked into several other forces.

I reverted to the toolbox and got a job as a maintenance fitter in a spinning company factory. I soon learnt that Navy way of doing things and civvy way were very different. I expected to be at work on time and finish a task before taking a break, especially when dealing with a breakdown. The other guys generally arrived at the last minute and took time about starting to actually do anything and guarded their break times jealously taking more than they could as often as possible. They also had an attitude of us and them with the unions and management. It was not a long-term career option so very soon I moved on.

During this period, I was trying to think where I intended to go in a career. I had always been interested in working with or alongside the criminal justice arena. I considered lots of options, I had friends who were probation officers. I thought about being a Prison Officer, I looked at charities working with ex-offenders. And then saw an advert for staff at a probation hostel. I sent in the application and hey presto I got it. One of the benefits was that the job was residential, so I moved into a flat in the eaves of the building that was the hostel.

Then the problems started. I was totally out of my depth; I didn't know that young men could live the way they did and be so devious and dishonest. Give an inch and they would take a mile. When I was on duty, I was expected to check in all the residents in time for the evening meal, keep order through the evening provide an evening hot drink. Check that all residents were in the building for a ten pm curfew and that they were in their rooms by 10.30 pm. I then had to sleep in the duty room. I remember being shocked on the first night when I realized that the steel panels on the door were to protect me when I locked myself in and went to sleep. I was then required to wake everyone up and get them their breakfast before sending them out for work or to look for work. It was when I found out that one of the residents was supposed to do the breakfast prep, and that the Manager, was according to the books, paying one of the residents but was pocketing the money. That was when I decided to leave.

I worked for a short while in an employment agency and then took a job out of the box. This was working for Byam design, a company making point of sale equipment. I was the only full-time metal worker and the tools and equipment were in a terrible state. I moved on.

During the time at this last job. Janet and I were married and bought a house in Wigston. So changing jobs was a big issue. I had to earn a reasonable salary or wage.

On the first Monday out of work, I was out on my motorbike looking for work. In those days factories looking for staff used to put a "vacancies" board up outside. I was driving past a factory and saw that they were looking for staff at several levels. I went in and asked how much they were paying the bottom category which was as cleaner / operative. When they told me it was more than I had been earning the previous week, I asked for an application form. When they read it, I was asked if I wanted to actually apply for a job as a semi-skilled engineer as I had the qualification for that position and it paid more. I filled in another application form, they called one of the engineer managers down to interview me and take me round the factory. After the tour He asked me if I would like to apply as a skilled engineer as it was obvious I had the necessary skills. And that paid even more.

I started work as a skilled engineer on the production line making "Fairy Liquid" bottles. The company, BXL made all sorts of plastic bottles, by the thousands, 3 shifts a day 5 days a week. The first week I was doing days for company induction training. The next week I was on the 2.00 pm to 10.00pm shift, at the end of the second week I received my first weeks' pay package and thought it was wonderful. The following week I worked from 6.00am to 2.00pm and at the end of the week got my wages for the previous week. That had been on shift hours so in addition to normal salary I got a shift allowance which was even more. It seemed each week I was being paid more. Then the fellow who was my shift leader asked if I would be interested in moving up to shift leader as he was being promoted, so I said yes. One problem was that another shift leader had left so there were now only 2 shift leaders until they could recruit a third. So could we work 12-hour shifts. Which paid more and when doing a twelve-hour night shift was paying huge amounts of money. When I left my previous job, I had been earning £40.00 a week but now, only 4 months later, I was earning in excess of £300.00 per week. BUT money isn't everything and I was absolutely exhausted. Family life was non-existent, and it was just wrong.

I took some time looking for another job and found a job as a buyer for Bentley Engineering, a company making circular knitting machines. It was a real change of environment I had never really worked in an office before and some of the procedures and processes seemed strange. Remember this was before we had any computers in the office. Initially I was responsible for the purchase of consumable tools and steel bar materials. I was able to save the company several thousands of pounds a year on the purchase of tubes after one supplier offered me a bribe of £100 to keep giving him the business. We used to get requisitions from the tool store or production office, so that we could place verbal orders with our suppliers before sending a typed purchase order. We only had one typist for 5 buyers in the department, how she managed I will never understand. Occasionally we had a backlog of orders to be typed and the goods had arrived and been paid for before the order was ready. After a year one of the other buyers moved to another department and I was asked to take on the purchasing of all raw materials. But give up the consumable tools until the new guy had got a handle on it when he would then also take on the bar stock materials. He never took it on and I ended up as the materials buyer. I was placing verbal orders for the production of tons of materials, some orders of a value of several million pounds. It was an awesome responsibility at the time.

I really enjoyed the work and was hoping to improve my position and earn a better wage but the only way that could happen was to get a promotion. My Immediate boss, George Law, was a few years away from retirement so was going nowhere. The head of department, Ralph Stacey, was in his 30's and seemed set for life there and anyway that was 2 steps up. So I let it be known amongst my suppliers that I was looking to move on. Within a week I had been offered a job with a tool supplier at almost double my current salary.

A few weeks after I started at the new job, I went back to Bentley's to see the staff and was advised that Ralph had left and that I could have had his job. It was probably the biggest mistake I made at that time.

I assumed that the job at Cromwell's was similar to the job at Bentleys, but nothing could be further from the truth. Mick Gregory the founder and MD of Cromwell's was the only negotiator for the company, so all the buyers were in effect order placing clerks. With a set procedure for the purchase of each Item. Each day we received all the orders and requisitions for items and itemized them on a list then worked through the list ordering by phone what was wanted. It generally took two of us all day to complete the list, and then we started again. It was the most boring and repetitive job imaginable.

I lasted a year before getting a job with the manufacturing division of an advertising agency. We used to make plastic point of sale stands and equipment. The job was a blast and we had fun every day. One time some of the guys superglued the designers' pencils to his drawing board. To retaliate He cut a ¼ of an inch off the feet of another guy's chair, every day, until he could hardly see over the desk. On another occasion the bosses telephone was replaced with a Micky Mouse phone just before an important meeting, When he saw it the manager swept it into his desk draw so that the visitor couldn't see it. One of the other guys phoned him up so he had to answer it in front of the visitor. But the internal politics of the Managers meant that the company was barely profitable and in due time they "downsized "and I was made redundant. We had moved to a larger house during the previous 6 months. I was desperate for a job.

Ships are safe in harbour

But that is not where they are meant to be

Chapter 10

ROSS ON WYE 1980 - 85

Janet and I had married in 1976, Initially we lived on Little Hill estate in Wigston. We started to attend the Little Hill church and had good fellowship. We were involved in the activities and outreach of the church and thought we would be there for a number of years. We were living in a new 2-bedroom house, but when a 3-bedroom house on the same road came up for sale we put in a bid and agreed to buy it. We put our house on the market and sold within a few days. The vendors of the house we wanted then pulled out and left us with nowhere to live. So we looked around and moved to Homeway Road in Evington, Leicester. When I was made redundant from Composite Plastics we had been living there for about a year. Kelly had been born in November 1979 just a few months earlier.

Whilst looking for a Job I came across a government scheme that would supplement salaries for people willing to relocate to take skills where there was a shortage. The government paid a supplement to salary, travelling expenses until a move took place and all the costs of moving.

I got a job at Brooke Bond, in Gloucester and moved in as a lodger with my in-laws in Ross on Wye. Janet stayed in Leicester with Kelly, and I travelled home each weekend. This went on for several months. I would leave Leicester about 1.00 am on Monday morning to arrive in Gloucester in time for work at

7.30 am I used to get a fry up at the greasy spoon café near to the factory before work. Then leave work on Friday afternoon at the earliest possible time to get back to Leicester late evening. Eventually we managed to purchase a house in Ross on Wye on a new estate but then had problems selling the house in Leicester.

Eventual our agent suggested we drastically reduce the price and have an open day. We agreed to this, and my dad came to help. It was set for 2.00pm to 5.00pm on a Sunday afternoon. At 1.30pm a car with three men pulled up outside the house and the men came to the door. Dad told them we were not ready and to come back in ½ an hour. Spot on 2.00pm they came back. I started to show them the route around the house we had planned but the older man only wanted to see the toilet. He opened the toilet door, tried the flush, and told his colleague to offer us the money in cash which they had in a briefcase. Fearing the worst I told them that they should give the cash to my solicitor on Monday morning. Meanwhile people had started to form a queue to look around and we had some 30 people view in 2 hours. One couple seemed really interested and spent ages measuring up and telling me how bad my DIY decoration was and what they would need to do to put it right. Eventually they left. Several people said they would make offers to the solicitor the next day. We then collapsed with a brew and had some tea, before taking Dad home. Then we got a phone call from the last couple to leave. They would like to check that their VW camper would fit under the car port, so they came back, and I moved the car so they could try it. They were successful and in due course did make an offer and purchase the house. I was left to get a couple of hours sleep before setting off for Gloucester ready to start work at 7.30 am Monday morning. We did get moved and settled in Ross. A few weeks later we heard that the couple who bought the house had had an accident, and that the camper was a right off, it made me chuckle.

We started to attend the Gospel Hall in Ross on Wye. This was the church that Janets parents were members of and had been since they moved to the area 10 years earlier. We attended regularly but were not involved in any activities.

The job at Brooke Bond was working as a maintenance engineer on the tea packing machinery line. A couple of weeks after starting, another fellow and myself were taken off the line and we set up a separate workshop to revamp and recondition the machines. We had to strip them down to component parts then adapt them to add in a fault-finding sensor system. Then we rebuilt it and got it running to perfection. The first machine took about 4 months to do. It was great setting up a highly complex machine that worked to very fine tolerances at high speed. These machines used to make nearly a 1,000 tea bags a minute, not just ordinary tea bags but tagged teabags with a precise dose of speciality blend teas. Individually packed in an envelope. Having got them working and tested them for several days, we were then told to mothball them. We then started on the next machine, this one was a lot quicker as we had set up the workshop to do it and we had some experience. Of course, each machine we did was quicker, in fact we ended up doing each one in about 3 weeks including the testing. 6 days to strip and clean 6 days to adapt and rebuild and 3 days to test. But each one we completed was also one off the production line. When I first started working on the production line there were 30 machines all producing orders for UK. Then we got the order to prepare them for shipping overseas and those machines were sent to Sri Lanka for Brooke Bond to use there, where labour costs were much lower. It was obvious that the writing was on the wall for the future of that factory. By the time I left there were only 22 machines in the building and only 15 on production.

I decided to take out a franchise on a tool selling business, similar to the familiar Snap-On brand. I had a van equipped as a tool shop and travelled my area selling tools to local garages and anyone else who would buy. I had a regular day in each area and where possible a regular time at the bigger garages. I would then invite the mechanics to come out to the van to purchase items they wanted or at least to pay for products they had purchased previously. One of the factors of this business was selling product over a 10-week credit period. Sometimes one would find that people were not there to pay, they may be too busy to come out. Or just didn't want anything. There were two other people doing the same type of operation with different levels of price. I learnt a lot about selling or NOT selling as may be. Due to the unknown brand, it was a lot harder to sell the product and build the repeat business than was expected.

After I wrapped up the business another guy and I started an organisation in Ross on Wye to help the unemployed, in fact we were able to organise meetings to get advise groups to come and help and also to get funding that equipped and provided for a community workshop that ran for a number of years after I left the area.

Janet and I had started to drift apart and during this period it was exaggerated and often Janet would be off with her friends whilst I was left at home holding the baby, literally.

I was a total mess and knew things were wrong but had no idea how to deal with it. I knew Janet was in relationship with other men and was planning a life away from me. The business had been wrapped up, leaving me with debts and we had to move out of the house. We had acquired a dog and we moved to a house on a farm for a while. It was here that the real split occurred. I got home one day to find that she had moved into a bedsit with Kelly and left me the dog. I couldn't stay there long, so resettled the dog and found somewhere else.

At one point I was living in a rat-infested caravan with no electric lighting. Even now I have flash backs of partial memories of this period that do not make any sense. I know my behaviour and actions were irrational and unacceptable. As I write this, I am having problems putting things in chronological order. I do know that this was probably the lowest point in my life. I remember just weeping for hours at a time. I think if I had met some people at that point I would have been guilty of murder. I occasionally thought of suicide but couldn't decide the best way to do it painlessly.

I was unable to afford the legal representation I would need to contest the divorce. It was also apparent that there was going to be no reconciliation, so Janet could get a divorce after two years of separation anyway. We were divorced in 1983. She ended up marrying a fellow who we had first befriended when we lived in Wigston. He was, by the time they married, a Methodist minister and I should imagine she took to the role of wife of the manse very easily. Over the next year or so I saw Janet when I was able to take Kelly out for a day. But I have not seen her since then.

Peter Metcalfe one of the elders at the church offered me a house to live in. In was a terraced house in need of renovation. It had an outside toilet a Kitchen that comprised a sink with a cold tap, two reception rooms and three bedrooms. There was no insulation or heating. I had some furniture and managed to make it reasonably cozy in a camping sort of way.

I also got a job at Gloucester Cathedral school as a workshop technician. I looked after the workshop and prepared materials for the kids' practical exercises. After a few months one of the teachers had a couple of days off and I was asked to supervise the workshop whilst the head of department was in the adjacent classroom taking both classes. I started to help some of the kids and gradually I was encouraged to take on the role of teacher in the practical area. One thing I enjoyed was demonstrating left-handed to left-handed kids and seeing them actually enjoy doing practical tasks, because they found it easier to visualise from the demo. During the quiet times I managed to make a couple of easy chairs and a coffee table which made the house more habitable.

My head of department, Stan Cooper, was also in charge of the school sailing club, and it fell to me to maintain and service the club dinghies and safety boat. I enjoyed this and think I made a decent job of it, sufficient that I was invited to attend the school sailing camp at Rock, in Cornwall, we were camping in a field just up from the harbour and I spent most of my time operating the safety boat or the shore safety base on the beach. 2 weeks of joy. I have not actually done any sailing since those weeks back in 1984.

One thing that brought me back to an even keel was the friendship of the singles group at the church, Particularly Michael Spencer he was a mate who was just there, no advise, just there. I also started a simple relationship with one of the girls, Angie Criddle and we had some good times together, she actually took on the distribution of my prayer letters when I was on the Doulos, It was obvious to us both that this was not a long term relationship and we parted as friends during the time I was on the ship.

During this time, I had started to be involved with the activities at church and as described in the next chapter was challenged to get involved in Mission.

Chapter 11

MV DOULOS IN THE MED 1985

To recap in 1983 I was living in Ross on Wye, Herefordshire, My life was pretty desperate. Janet had divorced me, I had lost my home, and after living for some time in a mobile home that was infested with rats, I had moved into house owned by one of the church elders. It was in need of renovation, had an outside toilet in the yard, and a single cold water tap in the kitchen which consisted of a sink. The real advantage was that it was cheap. In fact almost free and everything I spent on improving the property was deducted from the rent I didn't pay. I had got a job working at a school but that was 15 miles away in Gloucester. Generally, I existed from day to day.

As we approached Christmas, the church elder who owned the house invited me and another fellow from church, Mike Spencer, to go with him to a Carol Concert on a ship and to have a meal afterwards. Free meals were hard to come by, so I jumped at the chance. Thursday 22nd December was a cold and wet day, we set off for Newport, Monmouthshire about 40 miles away. It seemed to take ages to get there and join the queue to get on board this old ship called the MV Doulos. Eventually we got a seat in a low-ceilinged auditorium almost at the back and could hardly see anything. It was probably the worst Carol Concert I have ever been to. They seemed to spend for ever talking about the ship, and where people came from. We didn't know the words of the unfamiliar carols and could not see them on the screens. A rather scruffy and gaunt fellow eventually started trying to pass out some ancient hymnbooks, but no one announced the numbers.

As I sat there, I was appalled at the maintenance standards of the ship, and wondered if there was anything I could do to help them get it improved. Then I found a leaflet saying that in each port they visited they accepted volunteers to help work on the ship. The concert went on for so long that by the time we left the ship and got on the road it was too late to get a meal. My first impressions of the ship may have been coloured by this but in any case, they were not favourable.

During the week between Christmas and New year Mike and I went to the ship again to volunteer and it was agreed that as teams from the ship were visiting our church on the following two Sundays, that we would fetch a team for the evening service and when we took them back to the ship we would stay on board and help until the following Sunday when we would take a team to church as we left and then return them after the evening service.

On Sunday 1st Jan 1984 I drove to Newport to collect a team to come to Ross on Wye for the evening service. Again, I was not impressed with what we got An OLD Canadian, A young Swede and another person. I subsequently got to know both of these characters quite well, Jack Friebel the Canadian was my mentor and friend for all the time I was on the ship and introduced me to Isobel. Anders Soderberg was on the ship when I eventually joined the ship and we have kept in touch over the years and are still in contact by Facebook.

After the service Mike and I took them back to Doulos and we were allocated a bunk each in a cabin. Next morning at silly o'clock I was woken by a fellow insisting that we got up to go for a run on the quayside. Not a good idea in UK in January, I declined to accept his invitation at which he seemed to get very insistent. Mike seeing this surfaced and suggested in a very polite way that if this fellow wanted to see breakfast time he had best go away. Those who know Mike will realise that he is a BIG aggressive looking chap, so the fellow left at great speed.

Breakfast was a shock, it was some sort of porridge, that was tasteless. After breakfast the volunteers joined the crew for devotions and then met in a classroom for further training in evangelism. I realised that that was not what I had volunteered for so made representation and was introduced to the first officer George Booth. He took me and got me working with a gang who were rebuilding section 6 of the ship as accommodation cabins, It was something I was used to and I enjoyed the work and mixing with the crew, I worked mostly with a chap called Jeff Cranage, he was an American, but a good guy for all that. During the week the 1st officer, George Booth, invited me to consider joining the crew for a full two years. At the end of the week we took a team that included Susanna

Molina and Dora Cordenas back to Ross for the Sunday. Whilst enjoying Sunday Lunch after the service Susanna noticed it was snowing outside and rushed out to see what it was. She very quickly ran back in saying "it's cold" she had never seen snow before.

The ship sailed from Newport a few days later taking Mike with it. He had signed on as volunteer whilst the ship was in UK. He worked in the engine room and Johannes Thomsen the Chief Engineer appreciated his work very much.

But a seed had been sown. Getting the news from the ship and OM kept the idea watered. One project that we heard about was that the ship was collecting second-hand books that they could take to Africa and sell at a nominal price, so they were affordable in developing countries. Our Church decided to support this effort and we collected second-hand Christian books. In March 1985 Mike and I took a vanload of books to Southampton where Doulos was then berthed.

I had until then just got on with living, I had developed my position at the school and was now doing some teaching, things were getting better materially, and I had put thoughts of joining Doulos on the back burner. However, even in the 24 hrs Mike and I stayed on the ship we were impressed again and encouraged.

Back home in Ross on Wye I attended a church prayer meeting. The theme was about fulfilling our commitments. After a while I was no longer taking any notice as I debated with God. How could I go? Where would the money come from? What about my recent, personal history? What would I do? Could I not just put it off until another year or two? By the time the meeting was over I was in no mood to speak with anyone and just headed home. But I got no peace, so I made a deal with God, LOL. If OM would accept me, I would go but He had to provide the finance. I wrote to OM and went back out to post it that same evening before I changed my mind.

You will not be surprised to read that in due course I left home to join OM. I had seen God open the way, provide me with resources and finance, supporters and prayer partners. And taught me that as I gave, I received. I remember the Saturday toward the end of July 1985 when I travelled to a school in Bromley, Kent to join a group travelling to Belgium for the Summer campaign conference. I spent most of the journey having a real good laugh with a young lady. My abiding memory of her was her revelation that she had been "cashiered from the Brownies, for kicking the toadstool" Of course this was before I had learnt the Social Policies of OM.

We arrived at Belgium Bible Institute in Leuven, Belgium, having travelled over the channel by Hovercraft to Boulogne and then travelled to Calais by bus to pick up more people. It was getting late by the time we arrived. The fellows were allocated a space in a cavernous half-built space with homemade beds that doubled as storage for our luggage. There were probably 100 fellows in that room. One soon learnt about the foibles of one's fellow man. During the following week we were trained in evangelism and the ethos and principles of OM, and selected for the place we would spend August doing evangelism. Although it was a requirement to speak German to go to Austria, I persuaded the leaders to allow me to join a guy's team working to the north of Melk. One day we were going out visiting houses door to door. There are many hazards and difficulties in visiting house doors, we all know about the postman and the dog. As we approached one gate we could not gain access and pushed the intercom button to get the gate opened. No response so we looked over the top of this high gate only to see a Camel looking back at us and spitting in our general direction. I am afraid that family missed out on our visit. Never the less during our time in Austria, I found that I was able to share the gospel with someone each day, without speaking German.

For my last weekend in Austria I was privileged to visit Vienna to help with driving some trips for the OM team based there. I then travelled back to Leuven with a fellow called Bryan Grey, we were driving a Citroen 2CV and did the journey in about 12 hours absolutely astounding.

We spent most of the month of September being trained and inducted into OM and prepared for joining the ship. During this time I made friends with a chap called Steve Packwood. It transpired that his father was cousin to my brother's wife. Before joining the ship, we were sent back to our home churches to advise them of our plans and to get their support for the future and then we reported to our home country HQ. OM UK had recently relocated to the Quinta in Oswestry, Shropshire, When we arrived we were told that we could not move out to the ship until OM had settled all the previous year's bills and that they were and we were, praying for the money to come in. Whilst we waited, we were set to, working on the grounds and doing maintenance around the buildings. It did give us time to get to know others who were joining the ship at the same time. The gathering included Anita Browse, Caryl Davies, Debbie Forrester, Steve Packwood, Jim Pugliese, Simon and Liz Coward, Hossein Fahabian and a few more.

Eventually the day arrived, and a coach came to collect us to take us to the ship. It was supposed to be a luxury coach with a fitted toilet, but it didn't actually have a toilet. A group of us got on the coach and we travelled to Bromley in Kent, OM International HQ, where some left the coach and others joined before we went to the ferry in Dover. We pooled our money and bought a packet of chips each, the only food we had all that day. At Calais some more left the coach and other joined. Then we continued to Paris to the OM France offices arriving at about 2 o'clock in the morning. The team there gave us soup and bread again some left and others joined the trip. The coach continued and at lunch time we stopped at a roadside cafe and had a meal that the coach organiser paid for out of money given him by the office. On we went until we arrived at the Spanish border, which in the days before European Union was a customs check point. We had a case of pharmaceuticals on board and several people with uncertain political status. The coach drivers expected this to be a difficult crossing and had made plans to bribe their way through with a packet of Cigarettes being available for the guard to pick up. We decided to pray our way through. When the guard came to check he walked down the gangway and looked at passports then he stopped looked to the back of the coach where the pharmaceuticals were and several of the "difficult" passports were sat and either decided to go no further or did not see anything. He then got off without taking the bribe and waved us through. It took just 20 minutes. We continued on our way and arrived in Barcelona at the ship at 8.00 pm having been on the road for 36 hours and having only had 2 meals in all that time. We found out afterwards that OM had paid for a luxury coach and given money for us to get food but that the person organising it had pocketed the money he saved by not supplying what he should.

I had said privately to God that I would go anywhere, do anything he asked except, share cabin with a German or go to India, the white man's grave. I should not have been surprised having been in Austria with 3 German guys to find when we arrived at the ship on a Thursday night that I only ever shared accommodation with German brothers. Most of the next day was spent in orientation and starting in work departments. Come Saturday morning I found myself on the list of those going out in evangelism, Jim Pugliese and I were told to go door to door to sell books and invite people to the ship, But neither of us spoke any Spanish and the fellow we were with was Portuguese, Although we tried hard I don't think we made any significant difference. This experience persuaded me to get involved in ship visiting ministry to other ships in the port, which I did for most of my remaining time on the ship.

I soon settled into a regular ship routine, I worked in a department for most of a working week, but also was involved in a study group programme, got involved with church teams generally on Sundays as well as helping with onboard programmes and half a day a week of evangelism. I was working in the engine room department involved with air conditioning and welding, and other engineering project work that was going on. I worked with some of the best guys, Jack Friebel was the plumber, with Paul Mitchel as his mate, Randy Jury was the Welder with Carl Wilson, Mark Dimond was the engineer in charge of our departments, and we are still in touch to this day. After a few days the ship moved down the coast, a few hours, to Tarragona. Where we stayed until 13th Nov 1985. When we sailed for Genoa, Italy,

I had trained in the Royal Navy and was used to working at sea and resting and playing in harbour. So,

I was a little surprised when on the first morning at sea I arrived at the workshop, only to find it locked. I had never needed a key before so didn't know who had one or where it was kept. But eventually found one and was able to get on with work. Come coffee break and I headed to the crew mess, where those in overalls could sit and get food and drink. Usually the place was full at break time but that day there were perhaps 12 guys rather than 40. I realised that quite a few deck and engine room guys had switched to watchkeeping routine whilst at sea but it still seemed empty. At lunch time just 9 guys turned up for lunch. The mess girl was sea sick, so sent away to rest, and the remainder of us sat down for a meal for 2 dozen. As I questioned the experienced guys I realised that on Doulos, Sea time is rest and recuperate time away from the public, That sea sickness was a real and actual problem for many, so unless it was essential jobs were just held over until the ship was in harbour. The other factor was that sat round the table of experienced guys the average extent of sea time exceeded 10 years.

In each port as soon as the ship could afford to, personal pocket money was given to crew members. We used this to buy little treats and luxuries that were not provided by the ship. Unfortunately this tended to be quite a small amount and may be as little as $2.00 per person per port, in local currency.

What happened was that people would accumulate money whilst in the various ports of a country that used the same currency. When we joined the ship in

Barcelona, Doulos had been in Spain since June and had visited 7 ports, so many of the existing crew seemed to have quite a bit of cash whilst us new guys had nothing or just a few dollars. In Genoa we were back on an even keel with the rest of the crew which was significant in integrating as one crew.

During these early days on the ship, I was privileged to make friends with a fantastic group of people. B G Cider from Sweden, Len Frayle from Canada, Stef Downham from UK, Kitty Pippin from USA, Debbie Forester UK, Anita Browse UK, Paul Young UK, Jaana Korkeamaki from Sweden to name but a few, in addition to those mentioned elsewhere. Many of these I am still in touch with 30 years later.

Genoa was also the HQ of the famous Costa shipping line and Doulos had been Franca C of the Costa line before OM purchased it and many people remembered it and visited. We got invited to visit their latest cruise liner which by comparison with Doulos was sheer luxury. It was also the port nearest the OM offices in Germany and UK that Doulos was going to visit for some time, so we had many visitors, including families of crew members. I had been allocated a bunk in a twin cabin with a German guy, whose family visited. They left him a huge stack of boxes of chocolates they had bought in Switzerland on the way. He kindly offered me free access to his chocolates, but I found it very difficult to just help myself. However this guy took offence and refused to speak to me, which in a small 2 bunk cabin was quite difficult. It was events like this that taught me much about people, culture and fellowship principles.

From Genoa we sailed to Messina. It was quite interesting to sail past the volcano of Stromboli whilst it was in one of its regular eruptions during one of the nights of that voyage. We arrived in Messina in time for some programmes before Christmas, only to find that evangelical Christians in Sicily do not celebrate Christmas. So that we did not cause offence we did not put up any Christmas decorations until after the last visitors had left the ship on Christmas Eve, Then the children on the ship put on a nativity play for the crew and received their Christmas presents. There was probably not a dry eye in the audience. On Christmas day the ship went out of routine and the highlight after a worship service in the morning was Christmas dinner served by volunteers so that the mess girls could relax and enjoy a break. Then after lunch was open cabins, due to the social policies on board It was a definite NO NO for guys to visit girls' cabins or vice versa, So an opportunity to socialise and see how the other half lived was great excitement, I spent most of the afternoon in one particular cabin but more of that later.

Doulos was waiting for a generator to be delivered and fitted onboard before it set off around Africa but there were delays in getting it completed so it was decided to do a few more ports in Europe and Doulos set off for Bari, and we arrived there on 30th December 1985. The ship held a service and prayer night on the 31st to prepare for the new year. It was interrupted at midnight as all the ships in the harbour set off rockets and fireworks to celebrate, everyone rushed out on deck to watch and wish each other a happy new year.

Whilst in Bari I went on a weekend team to Monte St Angelo further up the coast and on top of mountain. It was an interesting and exciting weekend living in a church hall on the edge of a drop of 1,000 ft down to the coastal plain. As we left Bari and sailed down the Adriatic we passed, what was then a closed country of Albania, so some crew members put Gospel tracts in bottles and jars and threw them overboard so that they might drift up on the shore in Albania. This may seem like a futile effort but recently I heard that someone had found one of those tracts which did lead to a changed life.

The ship sailed back through the straits of Messina and on to Naples, where we berthed at the jetty used by liners and cruise ships. In Naples we learnt that traffic lights on green mean stop because someone will be going through a red light across your path. We enjoyed lavish hospitality from locals and also American service people based there. We found out that the Mafia or Gang warfare is a reality. Having preached in a church on the Sunday morning a lady invited us to lunch, This meal took most of the afternoon and there was a likelihood that we would be late for the evening service at a downtown church where we were also taking part. The lady said she would get her husband (who didn't live with her) to take us in his cars, yes cars. They arrived in large limousines with curtains at the windows and we swept into town, ignoring the red lights. The husband asked about the ship and then announced that he would visit the next day "to check it out" When he dropped us off at the church the ushers were visibly shaking as they greeted us because we had got out of those cars. The next day the husband appeared on the ship and looked around and then told his henchmen that the ship was "off limits" We had no further problems with petty crime and shop lifting surprisingly.

A short hop down the coast took us to Salerno which was to be our last port in Italy. Here we received many truckloads of supplies sent overland from Holland that had to be manhandled on board. We also wanted to spend the last of our lira, so Steve and I with another guy went for a pizza in a traditional Italian pizzeria. All went well until we got the bill that seemed higher than we had expected and more than the money we had. Several senior staff from the ship were also in the pizzeria and one of them left us some money to settle the bill. But we wanted to pay what we had agreed. As we prayed for wisdom the place was hit by a power cut which shut down their till system, and when the staff came to ask us to pay they had to produce the bill by hand and not surprisingly it matched what we had expected and had the money to pay. As we settled the bill the power came back on. I learnt that even in physical small details God is in control.

Three days later we were waiting for the storms to die down so that we could sail into Grand Harbour in Valetta, Malta. We reflected how Paul, the Apostle, had been shipwrecked on Malta. In due time we sailed into one of the most dramatic harbours in the world. During the visit here the ships crew with the local evangelical Christians distributed a copy of the book of Romans in Maltese to every home in the country. We also took opportunity to get some relaxation on the beaches and enjoy the sights of a truly fascinating place.

We sailed on to Gibraltar. We were there from March 21st to April 8th. Our primary purpose in going there was to load the generator on board. This was a major engineering evolution which involved stripping part of the main engine away so that there was room to lower the generator into place. The engine crew set to and prepared the way, and on the appropriate day a lorry arrived with the generator on the back. A crane had been hired to lift it over the ship and lower it down into the engine room. Unfortunately, it had not taken into account that there was not sufficient room on the quayside to lift the load and then swing the jib round over the opening without the counterweights hitting the buildings next to the ship. Hasty reconsideration and planning had to be made. The ship repair yard, on the other side of the harbour, had a fixed crane capable of doing the lift if we could get the ship to the crane, of course there would be a cost if we had to berth the ship in the yard and it would also disrupt our programmes and so on. We had made preparation for the generator so the ship's engine was disabled, which meant we would need three tugs to make the move and only two were on duty standby. All this was going to cost a lot. As usual in this type of situation the ship crew were called to prayer, and God answered. A Christian naval officer who was the harbourmaster heard that we needed a third tug, so he called it out and with the two regular tugs transferred the ship across the harbour and back in one day as "a naval exercise" which was then paid for by the government. The gang of dockies at the ship repair company agreed to forgo their bonus wages to help the ministry. And the crane company returned their fee as they should have checked the space. By the end of that day the generator was suspended in the entry to the engine room, and we had more money than we started with. God not only answered he gave bonuses.

The next day it took all the engine crew all day to lower and manoeuvre the generator into its place. And the engineers started to reassemble the main engine. As we completed work that day we were told to get cleaned up and then gather in the crew mess. Johannes Thomsen the Chief Engineer then served us a steak dinner with all the trimmings as a thank you for a job well done.

By the afternoon of the 7th of April, the ship was ready to sail for Africa. Some Korean sisters went to their cabins as they suffered with excessive sea sickness, and they wanted to prepare themselves. Just before we sailed the port shipping agent came on board and told the captain that we could not sail because the bills had not been paid. Because of the time of day it was not until the next day that all was sorted out and we were cleared to sail. But during the night, the night watchman saw one of the Korean sisters running to the bathroom, and asked if she was OK. She replied that she was always sick at sea. He then told her that we had not actually sailed and were still in harbour. I can only imagine how embarrassed she was. On the 8th of April MV Doulos sailed for Africa.

He is no fool who gives what he cannot keep,

to gain what he cannot lose.

Jim Elliot

Chapter 12

DOULOS IN WEST AFRICA 1986

Due to anomalies in the worldwide fuel market, fuel was cheaper in the Canary Isles than anywhere else in the region, so Doulos called into Gran Canaria for a long weekend to take on fuel, arriving on the 11th of April. Initially it was not intended to carry out a programme for the public as we were only there for 4 days, but local pressure prevailed and a mini programme was produced. It was so popular that we repeated the international night on the Saturday night. I helped with stewarding the crowds and after the last event we were invited to a local family for a meal (stuffed squid). I think about 6 or 7 of us went, during the course of the evening they also invited us to attend their church with them the next day which we accepted. However, next morning, only two of us turned up to be collected, myself and Debbie Gohman. So off we went to church, then we were taken to a lady's house for lunch (stuffed squid), we were accompanied by the pastor's son to translate for us. After lunch we walked across town to an English girls' flat for afternoon tea. We had a great time. The next day I was summoned to the office and accused of breaking the SP rules, by walking out with Debbie. We had been seen walking across town during the afternoon. What they hadn't seen was the pastor's son, who they didn't know, who was with us and then made things OK. They also were unaware that I also had my eye on another girl, who our mutual friends knew all about.

As the ship included people from some 50 countries, we had developed an "International Night". A "show" that included such things as a national costume parade, cultural dances, music from different places and so on. This was then an opportunity to share the gospel from a view of diverse people with a simple faith in the Lord Jesus Christ.

Two tons of fish, donated by Korean Christians in an international fishing fleet, were loaded on board and we sailed for Cape Verde Islands and on the 18th of April we arrived at our first developing country of Africa, The primary language of Capo Verde is Portuguese so the voyage had been used to change stock in the book exhibition. On arrival the Pilot came on board as was usual, but he was, to say the least, inept and managed to crash the ship into the quayside puncturing the hull, in the process they trapped a guy on the loo in his cabin. Our captain ordered the pilot off the bridge, retook charge of the ship and brought us alongside. But the accident meant that I spent most of the time in Mindello working on repairs. One other thing that I remember was that the dock provided a barrel for our rubbish collection, we were used to having a skip but were reassured that it would be OK. We found this to be correct as every time someone took rubbish ashore a youngster would take it from them to put in the barrel but often it was recycled and spirited away before it ever got into the barrel.

The president invited the ship to visit Praia the capital when we left Mindelo, but we advised that we just could not afford the expenses of another port, to which he replied "I don't invite guests and expect them to pay" so we had a free one day visit to Praia.

Just one day later we arrived in Dakar, Senegal. The book exhibition crew had changed the books from Portuguese to French and we were at our first port of Mainland Africa. Senegal is a French speaking predominantly Muslim country which put a different perspective on the way we could do evangelism. For many of us it was the first experience of the poverty that we found throughout Africa. We also had opportunity to visit the island of Goree which was a slave prison that held slaves before they were put on ships destined for the other side of the Atlantic. What an evil slavery is, in the forms we know it from history and today. I found Dakar a difficult visit as I started to realise the problems, I had with not speaking other languages. One Sunday I was sent to preach at a local church with a small team as was the normal practice. We had with us a translator, but even so we managed to get lost on the way to the church and arrived late but we were very graciously forgiven. I then realised that the fellow with us to translate was actually Italian and I wondered how that would work out. But sure enough he was able to translate into French and we managed very well. It is a joy to say that Andrea Pappini became a good friend and still is to this day.

We moved on to Banjul in the Gambia, which meant a further language change to English. Each port had a different feel but what was apparent to us all was the desire for literature amongst the people even in their poverty. Most of us from developed countries had no concept of the reality of poverty but started to see it in person.

One thing I noticed in Banjul was the difference in culture with regard to retail. In most places the book exhibition suffered from small amounts of shop lifting. This became quite an issue in southern Europe until one of our electrical experts made a box with an old camera lens glued to it and a red flashing light that was installed to look like a closed-circuit TV camera. This reduced the pilfering quite a bit, but the amount increased again in Africa. Having checked that the light was still flashing we realised that the local people just didn't know what it was, and therefore ignored it.

From Banjul we moved onto one of the poorest countries in the world, Guinea Bissau. As the country was dependent on foreign aid there was some doubt that we could keep on the berth for the whole period, but we saw God overrule. We had expected that sales in the book exhibition would be low, but we were amazed, the most popular item sold was a pocket Portuguese New Testament, to spread the market, teams going ashore would take a box with them, and it was not unusual to sell them all before stepping off of the gangway. The ships leadership team decided to issue personal money to the crew so that we could put a little money back into the local community, but there was just nothing to buy in the shops. The Chief Steward took a van inland to buy fresh food and the only thing he could get was mangoes. Fresh mango, mango smoothies, mango chutney we had mango in every form it could be served. Along with the fish given by the Koreans in Gran Canaria in many forms. Food on Doulos was to say the least interesting.

Freetown in Sierra Leone was a fresh challenge. Captain Carl and his wife Marion were invited to attend the opening of Parliament and was invited to pray for the members of parliament. The President opened the book exhibition onboard with 5 vice presidents in his entourage. But at the same time the poverty just outside the dock gates meant that crew had to run a gauntlet of thieves and pickpockets so were advised to travel in groups of 6 or more. On one of the Saturday nights we had over 10,000 people coming to visit the ship and all men were called out to help with crowd control. It was a joy on the last day before the ship sailed to attend a baptism, in the sea at pirate cove, of two young men converted on the ship who were left in the care of a local church.

The president of Sierra Leone asked what he could do for the ship before it left and Captain Carl said "sell us some fuel at a good price, that we can pay you in local currency" this was because the exchange rate was virtually no use. OK said the president. Then started the story. It was several years since any ships had purchased fuel in Freetown, but there was fuel in the tanks at the other end of the docks. So on the last day before we sailed the ship was moved down the docks to the closest point to the fuelling depot. The pipes were connected up and the pumps were started, but no fuel flowed into the ship. The dock side workers then found that someone had stolen a section of the pipe between the tanks and the fuelling point. An hour or so later and a piece of pipe had been taken from another place and replaced the stolen bit. Attempt number two and the fuel started to flow into the ships bunker tanks. We knew how much money we had to pay the dock. And we knew how much fuel that represented. But the fuel kept flowing, we were starting to run out of space for more fuel as well as money to pay for it. The ships leaders sent out teams to sell bibles and new testaments on the streets to raise funds. An appeal was made on the ship to check if any local Leonies were still in pockets, wallets or purses. Every last coin was collected in. Eventually the fuel stopped, we could take no more, and the bill was presented and we could just manage to settle. Soon after we set sail for our next Port. After the ship had sailed that Mike Stachura the associate Director responsible for the finance, found some Leonies in his jacket pocket. He decided not to say anything at the time but told me about it at our reunion in 2017.

For most of the time I was on the ship, I worked in welding and plumbing department. As we set out to travel around Africa I was given a task of building an Air Conditioning unit to replace one that had been fitted on the upper deck back when the ship was a cruise liner. This unit was now well corroded and leaking refrigerant all over the place. I had the task of building the casing for the heat exchanger and also the trunking and casing for the Fan. We drew in air from outside and blew it through the heat exchanger and into the trunking that supplied fresh air to the dining rooms. Working without drawings or plans we managed to make all the component parts and to assemble them in the place provided. An electrician friend connected up the motor to the fan, and we went for lunch. As soon as we had finished eating, we were keen to check it was working and to bask in the thanks of the crew that the dining room was now Air Conditioned. So we rushed up and turned on the Fan. It went faster and faster and the noise it made got louder and louder. We realised that we had made the fan casing too tight and would need to re adjust it, so we turned it off and went back down to the dining room. Mayhem - apparently the noise down there felt even worse as it had reverberated around the room. Kids were crying and people holding their heads and ears. But even worse was that the fan had pushed air into the trunking and into the room, and that air had taken all the accumulated dust, debris, dead rodents and cockroaches and other insects and scattered it everywhere, Girls were screaming at spiders in their hair, The pantry girls were stunned at dirt all over the tables and one of the families were not too happy to find a dead rat on their table. It was wise to disappear for a while until things settled down.

The Doulos arrived in Monrovia, Liberia. Only to be arrested on berthing. The ship was in lockdown. Because the authorities had heard we were bringing "Secret Weapons" so they searched the ship and of course found nothing. But they did impose restrictions on our movements. Ship crew going ashore in groups of 4 or more had to take a policeman with them. So immediately every church team comprised 4 or more members so that a policeman had to attend a church service, The publicity also brought in larger numbers than expected.

When I first joined Doulos in Barcelona I met a young lady called Isobel, she was a feisty Scot who shouted at me. Over the coming months I got to know her quite a bit better, and occasionally managed to break the ship social rules in a mild way. The rules for starting a friendship with a member of the opposite sex were quite complex but also reasonable. It was expected that people would have been with OM for at least 12 months before asking permission. One had to ask permission and the approval depended not only on the people but the cultural rules of the countries that people came from. Before permission was given individuals had to literally keep a distance and always meet in mixed groups. After permission couples could attend devotions together have one meal a day together and go on church teams together otherwise, they needed to be with others or in larger groups. It was quite an event when it was published that this person had SP with that person. Most of their friends knew that it was on the cards so were not surprised but occasionally one was surprised. I had asked and the relevant events took place, and it was in Monrovia, Liberia that Isobel MacMaster and Lloyd Hodkinson had Social Permission, so had liberty to develop their relationship. To celebrate we decided to walk along the pier and get a drink (soft) before walking back, so taking a chaperone, Sue Owst, with us we walked to the dock gate and asked at a stall for a coke. This seemed a problem until after a while a man approached me with a small packet of white powder. I then had to explain that I wanted Coca Cola, not Cocaine. I think that this was the only occasion in my life that I was offered illegal drugs. A few days after we left Liberia there was a military coup, which we were very glad to miss.

Time at sea between ports was highly prized by the crew. Many people worked long hard hours dealing with the public, often not in their own language, which was very tiring so to have a few days break to rest and refresh was enjoyed by many. It was the nearest many got to a cruise. Some of the crew had to change their work patterns when at sea to keep all the sea watches necessary. But it did allow for some socialising especially when it was good weather.

The other thing that happened on this voyage was that the book exhibition changed language to include as many French language books as possible, as our next port was Abidjan in Cote d'Ivoire or Ivory Coast as it used to be known to the Brits. Along with the books on sale many of the conferences and programmes were going to be conducted in French. This meant that many of the crew had to work through translators who were in short supply.

Abidjan is a cosmopolitan, modern city with a strong French influence. I cannot remember why but the food improved tremendously. I know that Caryl Davis received a parcel from home that included English breakfast tea and Oxford orange Marmalade. And for some weeks the English contingent met for breakfast of tea and toast on a Sunday morning. BG also got a gift from home and went and found a supermarket in town that sold Swedish products and treated us to meatballs and Lingonberry sauce with Potato salad.

There was a big demand for teams to go to churches and a very full programme of conferences on the ship. When an invitation came into the ship for a Saturday event that appeared to be more social than spiritual all the main leaders declined going. Somehow it devolved to yours truly to attend. The invitation was for thirty crew members to have lunch with the Mayor of Abobo Gare a town about 20 miles inland from Abidjan. I was given the task of giving an after-dinner explanation of the ship and any other necessary communication with the Mayor. As previously mentioned, there was shortage translators, so Marian, the Captains wife said she would translate. The council sent a bus for us and as we were loading Marcel Georgel a French brother in the crew arrived back from shopping and asked what we were doing. He appreciated the translation problems and leaving his 2 year old daughter with crew members jumped on the bus to help with the translation. When we arrived in the town we found that the dinner was set out in a formal manner. Top table for the Mayor, Deputy Mayor, Assistant Deputy Mayor and the rest of the entourage, plus Guest of Honour, Translator and other guests. With the remainder of the guests interspersed with local people on further tables. Somehow although I was supposed to be the guest of honour I got put at the end of the table with one of the other folk off the ship. I was totally ignored by the 5th deputy Mayor who sat on my other side. It was however the first time I ever drank Pineapple Champagne, a never to be repeated experience. One can imagine the embarrassment when the Mayor stood and gave his speech and then I stood to respond and they realised I had been sidelined.

After the lunch the leaders of youth in the municipality took us on a walking tour around the town. Their intent was to show us things like the empty shelves in the town library. On the way they took us through the town central market, warning us to be careful etc. The group split up and made way through the market and as we assembled on the far side we realised that 2 of our attractive young ladies were missing, which caused a panic amongst our hosts. Who dashed of in all directions to find out if the girls had been abducted. Panic over when the girls were found blissfully unaware of the time and deciding which fabric to buy on one of the stalls.

A few days later our hosts responded to our invitation to them to visit us on the ship, where they told us that they had arranged for us to do an "International night" event in their town and that we were due at the TV studios to produce an advert that afternoon. We had no idea this was in plan and already some things were underway. That afternoon was my first (and last) interview on TV. The ship leaders told us that due to the heavy work load they would only commit 4 people to a team to go to that town. This was totally out with the vision of the organisers and almost impossible for us to do. So we asked for volunteers and eventually about 30 of us went to the event.

French speaking translators were hard to find at that time, Marcel was busy elsewhere, so we had a guy from Haiti assigned to us. We also took a local fellow with us, who had been helping on the ship doing some welding. Unfortunately, Abel had a stammer when he got stressed. On arrival at the venue we found that there were TV cameras set up for a live performance on a Saturday prime time show and that they were expecting 3 government ministers as guests of honour. As the programme progressed, our Haitian brother started to tire, and we asked Abel to take over for the preaching of the Gospel. As he started, stammered and one Government minister turned to another and said "Is this the best we can do?" I looked around and all of the team from Doulos were heads down in prayer. The next sentence that Abel translated was as clear as a bell and he didn't stammer for the rest of the evening. Over

300 people made a profession of faith in God that evening.

When we left Cote de Ivoire, we had to change languages again for the visit to Ghana. We berthed in the Port of Tema whish is precisely on the Greenwich meridian or 0 degrees of longitude.

We were very busy in Ghana with over 10,000 visitors on one of the Sundays during the visit.

During all of the time we were in West Africa the ship sent teams to visit churches and lead services on Sundays along with many other programmes and activities during each week. A team would probably be 3 or 4 people, One who would preach, another may lead music and the third share testimony. This varied and depended on the make up of the team. Generally we would be taken to the church take part in the service, enjoy some hospitality after the service and then head back to the ship. This also varied according to the denomination, and wealth of the church.

One Sunday in Tema I was leading a team that had an early start. We were collected from the ship by the pastor and a driver in a pickup truck and headed toward the area where the church was. As we arrived I realised, because the church had no actual walls, that it seemed the service had already started. However, we went and took seats. It transpired that the church met for 1 hour of prayer to start the day. Then held a 1 hour service with all the congregation that included preaching and teaching. For the next hour most of the church went out in small groups, door to door, sharing with people who lived round about the church. Converts were taken straight back to the church for the final hour of Praise and worship. The following week the new converts were given some basic teaching from the pastor during the hour of evangelism. And the next week they went out to share their new faith with their neighbours. The church had started with just a handful of members and less than 1 year later there were over 200 meeting each Sunday.

After the service, we went for hospitality with the pastor who lived with his family in a two room shack. After we ate the pastor took me to the second room which held a bed and a roll top desk. He had been given the desk by a missionary who was returning home. He used to sit on the side of the bed and do his study and preparation. His library of 7 or 8 books was very limited. When he visited the ship a few days later I thrilled to take him around and then give him a selection of commentaries, dictionaries and other study books that would help him in his work as a pastor. He and I managed to keep in touch for a few years, the last I heard the church had grown to about 500.

It was as a result of that meeting and seeing the need that I decided that supplying Christian literature was my work for the future. That was my work for about 30 years.

When the ship moved on to Togo we had to change language again. I have very little memory of Togo, except there was coup d'etat on the day we left. To sail on across the gulf of Biafra to Cameroon.

Most of the crew on the ship were volunteers for a two year commitment, and although people were coming and going all the time. Once a year was a significant crew change. This generally happened in September or October that fitted in with OM summer outreaches and conferences and also School and University terms. Some jobs and responsibilities on the ship tended to be given to 2nd year volunteers as they had gained some experience during year 1. So many people changed jobs.

Isobel was due to complete two years, whilst in Cameroon, but because we had started a relationship extended her time for a further period. I had been working as an engineer but in Cameroon I moved to the programme room. My role was to coordinate and run on board programmes. It was a bit of a learning curve but a very interesting and enjoyable role. When we sailed to Walvis Bay I prepared and organised a couple of conferences for the programme. And then started to prepare for conferences in Cape Town.

Statistics are like the varnish on a painting

Used to make things appear better than they are.

Chapter 13,

A PASSAGE TO INDIA AND BEYOND
1987

October of 1986 found the Doulos in Cape Town. I was working in the programme room organising conferences for the ship on board events. Isobel and I were getting to know each other better and the future seemed settled. The ships programme was to visit a number of further ports in RSA before heading to Tanzania and Kenya in east Africa.

I lead a team to a church one Sunday and was surprised at the lack of warmth in our welcome and I think it was the only occasion where we were not offered hospitality. A few days later I was leading a conference on the ship when one of the attendees spoke to me afterwards. He, Kurt, had been at the church on the Sunday morning and had wondered "….. if it was permitted" to take us for lunch? He explained that one of the church leaders was a bit "anti" so had advised against having anything to do with us. However, He would like to take us out for a treat the following week. "Would we be interested in a trip to Cape point to see the Penguins or a helicopter flight over Table Mountain?" It was a no brainer, so four of us were invited to meet up with Kurt and get a flight over the mountain and the City of Cape Town with the opportunity to take aerial photos of the ship. What a great experience it was.

I also needed to get new spectacles, as mine had been spoilt in a work incident. I managed to get a new pair of designer frames and good lenses and to this day do not know who paid for them. God provided in a special way.

A regular part of ship life was the ship prayer meeting, for which attendance was required. It was no problem attending but staying could be a test of stamina as it started at 8.00pm and could last until midnight or occasional until 6.00am the next morning. Over the years I was on the ship I saw answers to prayers on a frequent basis and enjoyed the fellowship with some amazing people. The normal pattern was to start with a time of praise and worship. Then move on into prayer for ship needs, individual's needs, world needs and any other needs, This would be interspersed with giving praise and thanks for answered prayer.

At the first prayer night in Cape Town, it was given out that there were plans being made for what happened after the time in Africa and that the plan was to go on to India. Before the ship visited a country or port, It sent ahead line up teams to prepare the way. Their job was to get permission for the ship visit and activities, often in hostile circumstances. Their second job was to work with local Christians and churches to develop a programme for the visit and finally to publicise and promote the visit, so that folk would know we were coming. The ship leaders then said they were looking for people to go to Bombay (Now

Mumbai) to do the Line-up as it was known. The team would be leaving from South Africa to travel to India.

I had a distinct feeling of God saying, this is for you. But, Isobel had just extended her stay by 6 months of which only one month had passed, I didn't want to go to India. I did want to see more of RSA and East Africa. And what did I know about line up. I spent most of the night thinking about and praying for guidance about this. Isobel also did likewise. I felt I needed to speak to one of the leaders about this and on my way met with Isobel who told me she was happy with whatever decision we came to. When I met with Alan Adams and Mike Stachura the conversation went something like this.

> *Me – "I feel God is leading me to volunteer"*
>
> *Them - "Good you're one of the guys we had in mind, as you are the most suitable for it "*
>
> *Me – "When will we be going?"*
>
> *Them – "next Wednesday"*

That was just 5 days away and was in fact unattainable but 12 days later we were on our way.

To compensate for the short notice and the extensive separation the ship leaders gave a dispensation and allowed Isobel and I to go out on a date alone. This was contrary to the social policy described in the last chapter. One of the leaders recommended a restaurant and made sure we had enough pocket money to afford a restaurant meal. The ladies got together and sorted a suitable wardrobe for Isobel and managed a hair do. Another leader made sure we had a vehicle to use and put some fuel in it. It was the first time we actually went out alone.

A few days later Kathy Kam Chin, Graham Wilburn and I flew up to Nairobi, we had to go there to get visas as this was the latter days of Apartheid in RSA and India had no diplomatic relations with RSA. We stayed in the Wycliffe Bible translators for 2 weeks whilst waiting for the visas. And then flew to Bombay.

Arriving in Bombay has to be experienced rather than described. Heat, smells, dust and people everywhere. Fortunately, we were met by one of the OM team in India. K J Johny who took us to the OM residence in Nana Chowk. And immediately took us to the Golden Crown Restaurant/ Café for some lunch. The waiter put 4 glasses of water on the table before he took our order. Graham and I both lifted the glasses and chugged them down, at which point Johny said *"Here in Bombay we do not usually drink the tap water"* Sure enough, nature took its course, and shall we say that neither of us strayed far from a bathroom for a few days. Welcome to India.

We soon got into the process of doing our line-up, and there were many interesting stories around that as well as strange things in our free time. Being advised to catch the number 78 bus only to find that the number displayed on the bus was in an Indian script that I couldn't read. Waiting for two days in an office only to find that it was the wrong office. Visiting the Dharavi slums, at that time the largest in the world. Preaching at a church with over 3,000 people attending. Sharing the gospel in a hovel with 3 beggars from the streets. Sacred cows walking the streets. Being held up in the street and being rescued by the staff from the Golden Crown who we got to know well. Using my experience of blending tea for Brooke Bond to make friends with our shipping agent. I could probably write a book about my experiences in Bombay.

After 3 months in Mumbai we were approaching Christmas, teams were starting to come to join us so that they could then proceed to other cities around India to do the specific line-up for those places. As Christmas day was a public Holiday we decided to find a restaurant where we could get a traditional Western Christmas dinner. We checked the menu and booked a table. What a superb meal it was, until we got the bill which was 3 times what we had seen when we booked. The proprietor then told us that it was higher priced because it was Christmas. Check the small print and make no assumptions when in Bombay.

Of more significant interest toward the end of our time there we still needed to get a bank account for the ship and visas for all the crew from multiple countries. We eventually decided that the only option was to actually go to the government offices in Delhi in person. Problem was we had no money to get there. We used to get funds brought to us from the Ships office in

Germany, but we had had to make some payments and also need our living expenses etc. We needed 2,000 rupees for return fare for two to travel. And we could stay at the OM residence in Delhi. Apart from our monthly team allowance we sometimes received "expenses" for preaching when went to different churches. On the critical weekend before we needed to go, we spent some time in prayer and alerted the need to other teams in OM. Sunday morning, we met again to pray and then the three of us went our separate ways to visit with different churches. On our return to Nana Chowk we met up to discuss our coming week. Graham said he had received a gift at church of the normal 200 rupees. Kathy said she had received the same and I glanced at the cheque I had been given and said I had received the same. Until We looked at the cheque from the church, I had been to which was for 2,000 rupees. The next day we booked our seats and by the Wednesday after a 12-hour overnight train journey we were in Delhi. The way was opened up for us to get the documents and permissions we needed, and we were back in Bombay by Saturday morning.

The following week were all in our office at Nana Chowk when a police car pulled up outside and a police constable came in and told us that we had to report at police headquarters the next day at 2.00 pm. Everyone was worried that we may be arrested and deported so we packed our belongings and passed all our information to Indian brothers so they could continue the work if necessary and duly presented ourselves at the police HQ.

We were taken to a waiting area and only a few moments later were told to go into the office. Inside the Commissioner of Police for Maharashtra State offered a seat and asked if we would like tea. Then told us that his wife, a Christian, had heard about the impending visit and urged her husband, a Hindu, to support our visit. Suddenly we were able to arrange for access for the public to secure areas a police guard for the ship (for free) and visas for all the crew including a Pakistani brother. He even came as the guest of honour to perform the grand opening of the ship to Bombay.

We were nearly 6 months in Bombay and saw God move and change circumstances. Provide people and resources time after time. It was a life changing experience in many ways

Early March of 1987 the ship arrived in Bombay a few days earlier than expected, because the previous visit to the Seychelles had to be cancelled. I think the only person glad that the visit there was cancelled was Isobel as we were reunited sooner than expected. That night, against all the rules, I proposed, and she accepted. Then we went to the Golden Crown to celebrate.

The visit to Bombay proceeded well and was quite a busy time for the crew, but most managed to get some time off to see the sites. One day a sister from South Korea, Prisca Ahn, went shopping with a local volunteer and as she got on a crowded bus slipped as it moved off and fell into the road, banging her head and being concussed. She was taken to a local hospital which could only supply rudimentary care. The ships doctor was soon on the scene but there was little he could do whilst she was unconscious. Indian hospitals do not provide food and only basic care so the numerous nurses on board went to the hospital and nursed and cared for Prisca round the clock. Unfortunately, she went to be with her Lord and Master after a few days. Her family back in Soth Korea took comfort that she was cared for by loving sisters in last hours. Following local practice, the funeral was held the next day in a large church in Bombay. Several eminent church leaders from different groups, who had not spoken to each other for some time because of differences, met at that funeral and some reconciliation occurred between them. Even in her passing, Prisca was instrumental in building the Kingdom.

We sailed from Bombay to Mangalore, it was a pleasant 3-day trip that allowed for some relaxation after the work in Bombay. I helped complete the paperwork for Bombay and was ked to then move on to Singapore. We had a couple of weeks in Mangalore and then Isobel and I travelled up to Bombay, We had two days sightseeing before we went to the airport and Isobel flew back to UK whilst I caught a flight one hour later for Singapore.

I was met at Changi airport and taken to meet the folk where I was to stay. Ken and Bee Lee Gan, the leaders of the line-up team who were Singaporean were already in Singapore. I was staying Rodney and Irene Hui. Rodney was the team leader for OM Singapore.

The next day we had some orientation and visits to offices etc and the Kenny took us to the Cinema to see a movie. That night I felt ill, and, in the morning, Rodney arranged for me to see a doctor. I was immediately put in Quarantine with German measles. To cut a long story short, it was pretty difficult time with me being shipped pillar to post to less and less acceptable accommodation. And ended up in a Chinese style doss house that didn't even have doors on the rooms and living on MacDonalds breakfasts as it was the only food I could stomach. I was rescued by a former ship crew member who took me to her home where her mother looked after me until I was well.

The rest of the lineup was pretty plain except that I had to leave the country for at least 24 hrs to renew my visa, so I travelled up to Klang the port of Kuala Lumpar by train and then went back to Singapore to complete the arrangements for the ship visit.

The ship was in Singapore for a few weeks but toward the end of August I left the ship and flew back to UK in time to celebrate my parents Golden Wedding anniversary.

Why do we always find things in the last place we look?

Chapter 14

BROMLEY, URMSTON TO BOLTON
1987 - 90

I had come back to UK with 2 or 3 purposes. Firstly, I wanted to attend my Parents Golden Wedding celebration. Secondly I was changing field in OM from the ships to STL (Send the Light) and Thirdly or more significantly to marry Isobel.

We started to travel around meeting each other's families from Scotland to Berkshire, and Norfolk to Leicester. Isobel had a job as housekeeper at the Arran Outdoor centre where we subsequently held our wedding in January 1988. I also met with my sending church in Ross on Wye.

The Golden wedding in September 1987 was held in the same church building that Mum and Dad were married in 50 years earlier. They had been the first couple to be married after it was built and was the church we had attended before I was 5 years old.

I moved to Bromley where STL had their warehouse and offices with a view to working in one of their bookshops before taking over responsibility for their retail shops. After a couple weeks I was visited by the UK leader of OM who told me that my sending church had withdrawn their support *"because I was not overseas, and they wanted to support overseas missionaries"* This meant I could possibly go back to the ships or had to leave OM. But as OM wanted me to stay with them, they would lend me a house in Urmston nr Manchester so that Isobel and I could get married, join a church that would support us, so that we could continue in mission. It was another low point.

By this time we had acquired an old minibus with no seats in the back and was falling apart and I remember driving to Manchester to take over this house from the current occupants who were leaving the next day. I didn't even know how many rooms the house had, if there was any furniture. What I was going to do for income and how would we eat and pay for basic utilities. There was some basic furniture, and we bought a mattress from some money we were given as a wedding present. It was two years before we managed to buy the bed to go under the mattress.

After trying a number of different churches, we went to Chorlton Free church and that became our church during our time in Manchester. Early on we met Jim and Janet Barrie who were committed to evangelism and mission whilst they built their careers in surgery and anaesthesia. They very kindly gave us a car when they got a new one and it kept us going for a few years. They subsequently helped with our support for many years.

I managed to get a job as a Bus driver with the Bee line Buzz company. It was interesting but could be dangerous as a number of drivers were robbed and or assaulted whilst working. I was starting to feel the strain and after a couple of near misses and a minor collision felt that enough was enough.

Isobel had taken a job working in a Christian bookshop in Manchester but was finding the management style to be quite difficult. She heard through the grapevine of a position coming available to manage a new bookshop that was being started by a businessman in Altrincham. She was offered an interview on a Thursday morning. I took a days leave to go with her. As we went out of the door, the telephone rang. I took the call from the OM ships office in Germany.

> Them – *"Our new ship Logos II has broken down in the Mediterranean and is now in Gibraltar. We need crew to maintain and repair the ship so it can complete the voyage to Rotterdam. Would you be available for a couple of weeks?"*
>
> Me - *"When do you need someone?"*
>
> Them – *"Tomorrow"*
>
> Me – *"If Isobel is offered the job today with sufficient level of salary I will let you know if I am available tomorrow."*
>
> Them – *"OK, we will be praying."*

Isobel got the job, so I rang the office and was told that they had arranged flights for Monday. I gave in notice to Bee Line Buzz Co and went to Gibraltar. I was met at the ship by George Booth who had been chief mate on Doulos, and B G Cider one of my best mates. BG and I didn't get a lot of sleep that night as we caught up on our lives since we had attended his and Evvie's wedding in Sweden over midsummer. He was due to fly home the next day as he had already spent 3 weeks on the ship.

I found out that the initial problem with the ship was that a generator had had a significant failure and a second generator was not operational straight away. So they had had to be towed into Gibraltar. Over the weekend in trying to start the second generator it had also had a significant failure such that both of these generators were out of action. Safety regulations require a ship to have a number of generators capable of producing a set amount of electrical power. The ship had now dropped below that level so we would not be sailing until the generators were repaired.

I was able to stay in Gibraltar (on the ship) for 3 weeks before flying back to Manchester and home. I had given up my job, so we needed to see some extra income, that we calculated as £15 per week. In miraculous ways God gave us what we needed. I would get 1-day casual work and the pay was £15. We received an anonymous donation through the door of £15 another week. Final payment from Bee Line was £15 and so on. Some weeks we would get £30 then nothing for 2 weeks. I was helping as a volunteer in the Altrincham bookshop at other times. One evening as we returned home a stranger walked up to us and asked if the old minibus next to the house was for sale. It was not running so would need to be towed away. If we arranged the tow, it would cost us £20 or if we took it to a scrap yard we might get £15. I explained that to him and he arranged to take it away that night and gave us £60 or 4 weeks of our target. That was the last strange income we got as a few weeks later we rejoined STL and moved to Bolton.

We spent some time back in Bromley at STL HQ learning the ropes and doing a variety of work in different departments and getting to know the senior staff. During our stay it was announced that STL were relocating to Carlisle in Cumbria, and also that they were changing from being a "Faith Mission" to paying salaries for workers. In one respect it made things easier for us but…..

We moved into the flat above the shop in St Georges Road, Bolton. It was definitely a shock to the system. It probably hadn't been decorated in 20 years. The previous occupants had been 2 single guys, which was confirmed when Isobel opened the oven to find a tray of mouldy roast potatoes. It transpired that the last time they used the oven had been at least 3 months earlier. There were 4 rooms, on the top floor 2 large bedrooms, both with frosted glass in the windows, so one could not see out. Down on the 1st floor there was a lounge to the front, again with frosted glass, and a kitchen diner to the back, this did have clear glass in the window. One had to go through this room to get to the Bathroom, which was the only toilet in the building, so all of our volunteer helpers walked through our living accommodation. It took a long time to persuade the volunteers to stop allowing customers use of the facility. When we moved in there was just a curtain between the shop and the stairs up to the living accommodation. We had to turn off the alarm in the shop and go out through the front door of the shop even though we had a parking space in the yard at the back of the premises.

We looked for a new church in Bolton and after trying a few we started attending Cornerstone Baptist Church. The Pastor, Ron Stidham, was an American. He and Connie became friends and confidants very quickly.

An inconvenience we suffered was people phoning us after hours and asking if we had something in stock, and even if we could bring it with us to church. One Sunday afternoon I was in the bath when the phone rang, Isobel had gone out for a walk. I answered the phone, and the lady asked if I could just pop down to the shop and check if we had a particular greeting card in stock. She was shocked when I advised her that I didn't think I should stand in the shop window with just a towel around me. Or words to that effect. Needless to say we didn't take that card to church for the lady.

I never got on well with the Managing Director or CEO as he would be known today. Keith Danby took offence when I told him that I thought it was wrong to employ non-Christian staff in the warehouse. If I made any changes in either product or systems in the shop he was very critical, asking who gave me permission. He would then take the ideas and implement them in other shops. He never supported me when a customer complained that we had stopped keeping his magazine for him. He had had it last month so why had we stopped. On investigation the magazine had ceased publication over a year earlier. But it was still considered my fault.

STL retail was going through a reorganisation into the Wesley Owen group of shops and we were advised that the shop was not commercially viable as it was so we should be prepared to find something else.

Isobel was pregnant at this point so whatever happened was going to be traumatic. Gillian MaConway, a friend from the ships, was working at Bromley and put us in touch with OM's internal job vacancies, so we applied for a number of them. One was running a bookshop in Kuwait, another was literature coordinator for a team in Coventry UK. We visited Coventry, were interviewed and offered the position, Another was a deputation and recruiter for OM Canada working in the Atlantic Maritime provinces, As were going over to Canada to visit Isobel's Sister, we met with the team and they offered us the job, to the extent that they wanted Isobel to stay in Canada, whilst I went back and packed up ready to emigrate. Two of these offers asked for references from Keith Danby so I was summoned to Head Office and asked why I had the temerity to go looking for a job without asking him for permission. He then offered me another position that I did not think was suitable for us.

We also heard about a vacancy for a bookshop manager in Stamford, Lincolnshire. I had a picture in my mind of where the bookshop was and thought it might be OK. I sent off an application and was shortlisted for interview. On the way to the interview I stopped for a coffee and asked the waitress about directions, as a confirmation. (this was in the days of paper maps, not Satnav) only to realise I was heading in my mind to the wrong town. I did however get to the interview in time and was subsequently offered the position. It was arranged that we would start work after the Christmas and new year period. I gave notice to STL to finish work on Christmas Eve and vacate the flat between Christmas and New year. Our last day of trading in Bolton was the highest days takings for a single day and also the highest months takings ever. So much for being unviable.

Chapter 15

STAMFORD 1991 - 99

We eventually got settled into the house we rented in South Witham, with some help from my brothers and nieces and nephews, before the start day at The Ark Christian Bookshop. It was good to be making a fresh start with a situation that had some potential. And over the course of the first couple of years we were seeing many opportunities to distribute good Christian literature. We also had a small coffee shop, that was in retrospect just too small but a real asset.

Becki was born in March 1991 in Grantham. We were living at South Witham and not really settled in a church but did find fellowship with a couple of RAF officers who lived in the village and the local RAF chaplain who lived just down the road. The house we lived in was just 2 bedrooms Ideal for us with just 1 little baby. When Mark came along in 1993 things were getting a bit crowded. Roger, the RAF Chaplain, and Pauline his wife were posted to Germany So we moved into their house with 4 bedrooms, which gave us a lot more space.

Mark was born at Peterborough hospital whilst we were living in South Witham. A few days after he was born he would not settle at night and we spent all night carrying him around. We called the doctor the next morning and he visited an hour or so later. Then asked us to visit the surgery as his wife was the expert on young children. An hour later we were rushing him to the hospital to be quicker than waiting for an ambulance. Whilst taking details from us we were pushed out of the room as he was connected up to machines to do whatever machines in hospitals do. He was in intensive care and there was nothing we could do except go home to get some rest, and care for Becki. During the night I got a call asking us to go back in as they thought he would not survive the night. Isobel was exhausted, and what to do with Becki. So early the next morning we deposited Becki with Kimberly at Jean and Basil's house and headed for the hospital. Only to find that Mark was still with us and in fact as they had changed his nappy he had managed to wee over the machine and fuse it out of use. He suffered with respiratory problems for some years but seemed to get over it in time.

Things were going well at the shop. Sufficiently well that the trustees felt they could afford to appoint a deputy manager, so after interviews etc. Mary Sproson was appointed and became a valued colleague and friend. Her husband Paul was a computer expert in the relative early days of computing and suggested that we introduce computerised stock control and accounts to the business. We approached the trustees for permission to spend the money and I recall spending time trying to persuade them to spend more to get the 40mb version of a desktop instead of the 20 mb version. To put this into context, most smart phones have significantly more capacity than that first computer. Paul wrote the software, and it was better than some commercially professional software available some 10 years later.

We were supplying church bookstalls to places as far as Melton Mowbray, Oakham, Bourne and Market Deeping. During 1992 we took on a young Lady who was doing a gap year, Kimberley was developing work with a number of other bookshops where we put a consignment of our books on their shelves to extend our market. We also acquired a van so that we could go further in running occasional bookstalls at churches and other events in the area.

In 1994 Roger and Pauline were coming back from Germany so we had to move out and we bought a house in Garden Close, Stamford. Isobel was expecting Tim and with a young family we were starting to struggle with our finances. I used to get really concerned about things. One Sunday I was sent out of the house and told not to come back until I had got it sorted. I went to an Anglican church for the first time and was made welcome, I spoke with a number of people who I knew through the shop and some prayed for us. In a few weeks we started to attend at St Georges and got involved in the activities there. They took our ministry to heart, and it definitely became our church family.

It seemed we were constantly busy, especially with a young family. We adopted two elderly couples as honorary grandparents. John and Betty Bournon and Basil and Jean MacLennan. John was a retired Canon of the Church of England. It was an amazing privilege to be mentored and encouraged by that man of God. Basil and Jean were retired from their own family businesses and were, unknown to many, quite wealthy. We benefited from their support for many years.

As the years went by it was becoming apparent that the book trade was becoming more and more difficult. Making a profit was becoming more difficult. The Trust owned the historic listed building that we occupied so there was limited opportunity to extend or develop the building. Our Coffee area was just too small and because of enhanced food hygiene requirements needing to pay for someone to manage that area as well as staff for the shop it was just unprofitable.

We were also seeing the advent of computers for individuals, hence the name personal computer). In due time apart from the e-reader, which took a lot of sale of books. Use of overhead projectors and screens in churches, which meant reduction in sales of hymnbooks and Sunday school curriculum materials. Music went online so sales of Records, Cassettes and CD's virtually ceased over the years. The trade was starting into a period of change and decline which has continued for at least 30 years. How did it affect us in Stamford.

Some bookshops tried to diversify to deal with these issues, but we didn't have space for that. We attempted to link up with other independent shops in the area so we could enlarge our buying power to get a better profit margin from that. But it never really got off the ground.

Another alternative was to link with one of the larger chains of bookshops, so I wrote to three different groups with a view to then approaching the trustees with a business proposal. The SPCK group did not respond and closed down themselves less than 12 months later. Wesley Owen, the retail division of STL who we worked with in Bolton, wrote back and said it was not in their plan to take on shops at that time.

A few days after I wrote to CLC (Christian literature Crusade) I received a phone call from Phil Grant, who was the retail director, asking if he could come and visit on the following Thursday. When he and his wife Pat visited, we had a great time and an agreement to progress the takeover of The Ark.

CLC at that time was an association of missions working in about 40 countries around the world. It had been founded in UK in 1940 and spread around the world. At the time we joined there were approx 150 bookshops. The International Director, Peter Horne, was based in Sheffield. CLC UK had 19 shops and a wholesale department in Alresford. Over the next few months progress was made in the takeover. It did mean that we were going to close down the coffee shop area as CLC did not do coffee shops. Isobel and I would have to apply to join CLC and other staff would be made redundant. This was a difficult position as these were people for whom we had great affection.

We would also have to go through the CLC residential training course in South London for 3 months.

As members of CLC, which was a "Faith Mission", we would need to sell our house as CLC could not give us housing allowance to pay a mortgage. The absurdity of this is that we could move a few doors down the road to an identical house that CLC would rent for us, paying more in rent than we were paying in mortgage and also that upheaval. Jean and Basil MacLennan gave CLC the funds to buy our house so that we could stay where we were.

In due time we headed for Crystal Palace and the CLC HQ to start our residential training. Whilst this was going on the shop was still operating back in Stamford, so once a week I would travel back to oversee what was happening and try to keep things on track. Becki was only 5 and Tim was still in a cot, but with support of good friends we managed to complete the course. With memories being made. Neil MacKinnon asked at devotions one morning for a favourite song, Mark asked for Hickory Dickory Dock, so we all ended up singing nursery rhymes in devotions. All three of them asked the National Director of CLC if he loved the Lord Jesus before they would tell him where people were. Such a good time.

As part of the training course we went out on day visits to various other aspects CLC, one of which was a visit to the Wholesale department in Alresford, Hants. During that visit I really felt God telling me this is where I want you to be working.

A few weeks later we went back to Stamford with the intention of getting the shop going well under a new regime. A decorative makeover and a move of the office we reopened as CLC Stamford. The change meant we were getting better terms for our purchases and support with things like marketing and accounts. We managed to balance the accounts and start to make a small profit again.

One Saturday night I got a call from the police, that there had been a break in at the shop. When I got there I found that someone had thrown a brick through the big window at the end of the shop to steal the video player which was part of the window display. We needed to get the window boarded up whilst getting a glazier to come measure and refit the windowpane. As we could not afford to be closed on the following Monday we decided to clean up on Sunday. We needed to take every book off the shelves and check them individually as shattered glass splinters were spread throughout the room. Someone walking past the shop on the way to St Georges church enquired about what had happened and took a message to the rector. Kim Swithinbank made an announcement and immediately 6 people left the service and came and helped us clean up. We were able to finish by lunchtime, when we were expecting to work all day. It was an example of true fellowship at its best.

Computers were not so reliable back in those days, and in due course the shop computer crashed. I asked CLC to allow me to purchase a replacement but was advised it was not happening. We were the smallest shop at that time and even our London shop did not have a computer POS system. Instead of a computer they sent us a card index drawers and blank index cards. Fortunately, we had a fair number of volunteer helpers at the time. Roger Jones hand wrote every stock card, about 3,500 in total. Perhaps that is why when he, himself joined CLC he became the POS IT guru which he is still doing in 2024. CLC were good in many respects but like all organisations they were sometimes behind the times.

I was still convinced that we should move to Alresford to work on the wholesale side of the business and kept pestering the leadership for a move. Eventually I got a response that said they would allow us to move if or when they got someone else to manage the Stamford shop. The following week, late in the day, a couple who I knew came into the shop. After I had served them, I jokingly said If they fancied managing a bookshop there would soon be a vacancy. They left the shop but returned a short while later to ask for more details.

I think the leadership were a bit surprised when I found someone to take my place within a couple of weeks. Phil and Gina Inman were quickly accepted into CLC completed their training and took over the shop so that we could relocate to Alresford.

Chapter 16

CLC ALRESFORD 1999 - 2003

We moved to Alresford before the end of the school term so that the children could start at their new schools before the holiday. I started working in the warehouse, taking orders over the telephone, picking orders and packing them for dispatch to any of our 500 plus customers who all expected a next day delivery. It was physically quite intense, but a good way to get to know how the warehouse worked.

I found it interesting but realised that in many respects we were running behind the times. My immediate boss David Scott had been doing the job of warehouse manager for over 10 years and was due to step down in 12 months. The computer system was still the first generation that CLC had introduced and although it had been updated CLC were operating it as if nothing had changed in the first 5 years. They were also taking time to pack second-hand boxes with reclaimed packing with little understanding of the causes of damage to product in transit. Even the layout of the warehouse was not as efficient as it could be. It took me some time to learn these things.

The children had started at schools, and we looked around for a church. We attended the NFI church in Alton, but as I look back at it I found it a bit charismatic for me, but we did make some good friends there. Isobel was generally a stay-at-home mum. But did try to do some shifts in the warehouse answering the phone but found the computer interface difficult.

When I started at the warehouse, we were handling about 40 parcels a day and seemed as though we were rushed off our feet. We had a good team spirit but most of the team were getting on in years and finding the workload hard and change was difficult to accept. When David stood down from being warehouse manager, I was asked to take on his responsibilities. I have always understood that as a manager you need to make an impression early on and get the team on side. I decided on the first Monday morning to ask staff to take items they needed to keep out of the big lock safe so that we could clear the rest out to use it more efficiently. 2 people refused to do this but didn't say anything to me but went to Roger Page the Director, my boss, and complained that I was being "high handed" This was the beginning of a difficult 2 years.

I had asked when appointed if I could get some training on the computer system. It was arranged that Chris Weaver, the IT manager and I would do a three day residential training course at the Software company. I arrived at the premises on the morning of the first day, but Chris didn't appear and phoned in that he wasn't going to make it. So I went through the system training and found out that we could speed everything up with a few uses of the upgrades installed on the system. That there were a few hacks we could use to help better use and also a number of features that were available that would enable us to work more efficiently. When I returned to work I found out that Chris had told Roger that he didn't need the training as he was the IT expert. From then on I realised that whilst he was capable at his job, that those who "controlled" him had no idea so he had become "indispensable" This helped make my position very difficult

Gillian Scott, David's wife, had been the warehouse bookkeeper and when David stepped back she also left her job. Ann Wignall took on the role for a couple of years. But then passed it on to Roger Page's wife, Pearl. Roger could not allow Pearl to be under the warehouse manager as the previous incumbents had been so elevated her to Manager status, and in the process took away some of my status. The triumvirate of managers worked whilst Roger was there and kept his own responsibilities going.

In 2001 CLC UK were in conjunction with the international office opening a shop in Dar-es-Salaam, Tanzania and I was asked to represent UK at the opening. It was an interesting experience and re-awakened my love for Africa. I was going to have some involvement with Tanzania over the coming years.

When we received orders from customers, we would enter them onto the computer. Then print a picking list, that showed the location of the items in the warehouse. A picker would then take a trolly and the list and work round the store picking the items into baskets. They then brought the basket back to the workstation where adjustments were made on the computer, before a packing list and an invoice were produced. The basket was then taken back down the warehouse to the packing area where the items were boxed up and shipping labels attached it was weighed, for shipping costs then brought back up the warehouse for dispatch.

The first thing I fought to change, and it was a fight to make changes, was getting the picking list put in location order to minimise walking. This left the picker at the far end of the warehouse, so we moved the workstation down the warehouse so that they didn't bring everything all the way back And we built a conveyor system to take the tubs of product to the packing station. And on out to dispatch.

Next, we standardised the range of boxes which we got printed with our company logo to help keep us in the mind of our customers and we developed a better way of packing books into the boxes. All of these changes helped reduce the number of returns from damage and also speeded up the through put of orders. Whilst working with the same number of staff. We increased through put by 100%. We also started to include the weights of books in the computer system with the intention of getting pickers to put items straight into boxes as a start to the packing.

It seemed this was a step too far, as on one occasion when Roger was away, I made a decision that Chris Weaver and Pearl Page refused to concur with and actively went against my plans. On his return Roger supported their viewpoint and effectively sidelined my efficiency drive.

CLC UK at this time decided to start an online sales channel from the warehouse. The marketing was left in Chris W's hands and was never a realistic operation. So although the warehouse geared up and invested in packing and dispatching smaller individual orders we never sent out more than 10 items a day and often it was 2 or 3 a day.

During this period I did a 2-year course in management that led to getting Membership of the Chartered Management Institution.

Working with some of our suppliers of Children's books we started a scheme called Books 4 Schools, the concept was that for a donation of £100 an individual, church or other organisation could get £400 worth of books for a school library. This was a massive project for us and we saw thousands of boxes of books going into school library's.

I had realised that unless there were some changes in the senior group in the warehouse, I was just passing time, so when I was approached by Peter Horne the International director to consider joining a project to make affordable books available worldwide, I was instantly interested in finding out more.

Consideration was given to operating this project out of the Alresford warehouse, but as there might be space issues and potential commercial conflict. It was decided to start the operation in Sheffield, where the International Office was based. For several months I worked part time in wholesale and part time with Books 4 the World.

I was so disappointed that individual's sense of their own status had effectively stopped me doing a better job, 10 years later when I went to help out in the warehouse I found that they were still relying on some of the processes I had introduced and things didn't change until they relocated a further 5 years on.

Chapter 17

CLC INTERNATIONAL – SHEFFIELD 2003 - 2006

The plan was made for us to start the move to Sheffield. I was to travel up and find a place to live and a warehouse to work from. We were devastated before this process started to hear That Peter Horne had died whilst out on the Derbyshire hills.

The International leaders formed a committee under the chairmanship of Idris Davis to run IO until a new Director could be appointed. They decided to proceed with the project, so I started the process of moving up to Sheffield. It was not as easy as originally thought as we needed to find suitable schooling for the three, all in the same catchment area, a suitable house in that area which was convenient to where I had to find a warehouse/depot.

Looking for a 4-bedroom house within our price range was difficult and then finding suitable schools was the next issue. Good schools tend to be in more affluent areas where we couldn't afford the houses. The process stretched out over several months. We had hoped we could find an old church that had a hall or rooms we could use for storage, but that wasn't happening either. I can remember, as I was driving away from Sheffield one evening, thinking perhaps God wants us to move further out of town maybe somewhere like that (*pointing at a hill to one side*), as I went round a roundabout. I didn't know at that point we would live on that hill within sight of that roundabout for 13 years.

The next time I travelled up to Sheffield to view a few properties I was due to view one property and went to Aston but couldn't find the address. Remember this was before the days of Satnav. Then found out it was at Coal Aston, in Dronfield so a hasty rush across town and arrived slightly late to find the Landlord just about to leave. He showed me around what was just acceptable as a house and advised me where the local primary school was. He agreed to keep it vacant for us to get Isobel to visit a few days later. I visited the school which was also acceptable. A quick rush down to Hampshire and back up 2 days later with Isobel and the family to view and also visit the primary and secondary schools.

We eventually moved in June 2003.

At that point we still had no depot. Until one day a colleague heard that a Christian businessman in Chesterfield had just let his premises. We jumped in the car and went to see him to find that the premises were still available, and we left with an agreement that we would rent the place.

When publishers publish a new title, they estimate how many they think they will sell over a period and order that many books and calculate all their costs and retail prices on the estimate. It is good for the publisher if they can add an extra quantity to their estimate and reduce the unit price, or sell the whole extra print run-on at a lower cost price. We at B4tW were going to buy those print run-ons. We would also buy remainders from publishers who had estimated their print run too high and had surplus stock to get rid of. We also had some mission minded publishers who just gave us best possible terms so we could sell on these books to Developing World countries.

We soon set up a website and started sending books in bulk around the world.

In the process of extending our stock range, we approached The Alpha Course to see if we could distribute their books around the world. I was invited to a conference at Holy Trinity, Brompton and there I met Stephen Kimbowa from Kampala, Uganda. We thought it would be a good idea to find someone in each country who could run a bookstall supplied by B4tW. So when Stephen invited me to visit Uganda I was only too pleased to go. Stephen became a real good friend over a number of visits and we were able to supply him with a stock of books for him to sell on. Uganda is a beautiful country and with Stephen I visited the Equator and also the source of the River Nile. I wonder if the plastic duck I set in the water has made it to the Mediterranean yet.

We had had an enquiry and order for some books from a lady in Kenya, she asked if we could meet when I was in Kampala. I wasn't able to travel to her but suggested that if she came to Kampala, I could see her one Saturday afternoon. I had looked in the Atlas and saw that Nairobi and Kampala are only about an inch apart so it shouldn't be too hard. Its not until one sees Africa that one understands how big it is and how long it takes to travel on the poor-quality roads. This lady caught a 12-hour overnight bus so that she could come and meet me. That is how I met Kentice Tikolo, a lady who had a significant part in the next stages of CLC in Africa.

One of the customers who responded was based in Lagos, Nigeria. I was encouraged to visit Nigeria for a trade fair. He and I signed an agreement for the largest order we had received to date. We shipped 5 pallets of books to him at our expense. Unfortunately, He never paid for them and it left a large hole in our finances which we were never able to recover from.

Whilst we were trying to get our payment we continued to operate in several ways. We ran a training day for people interested in running a bookshop in Africa, and one couple who attended lived in Sheffield but wanted to open a shop in Zambia. In due time they asked if I would go to Lusaka to survey the feasibility of opening a shop there. Fortunately, they paid for the flight and arranged accommodation for my stay. When I arrived at Lusaka airport, I was having small problem with immigration when a smartly dressed man appeared and waved his ID to the officials and swept me through to his chauffeur driven Limo. He introduced himself as my host and told me that he was an MP and Government minister. He took me to his home and installed me in the guest wing. The next day we went on a tour of Christian bookshops etc in the area and discussed the possibilities. Then he told me that he was going to be busy for a few days and left me a chauffer driven BMW for my use during my visit.

It was quite a new experience for me especially when he wanted to take me for Sunday lunch in a hotel with his family and the security guys checked the restaurant out before we were allowed out of the car. I felt like royalty even though the food was terrible. Unfortunately, they were not able to raise the funds necessary to start the work in Zambia.

To go back to Kentice. She invited me to visit Nairobi, Kenya which I was pleased to do. On my first visit Kentice took me on a tour of the various Christian bookshops in Nairobi and introduced me to a number of influential people in the trade. At one point in the tour, we were in the compound of an American charity, who had imported a slice of America for their people to live in. As we walked round the compound we could see a lot of shanty dwellings outside the compound. I asked Kentice which side of the fence she came from. It transpired that she had been brought up in a rural village. But I will never forget her next line. "I have experienced poverty, after all I have been to Glasgow" She had got her Masters degree at Stirling university.

My conclusion from the visit was that although there were a number of successful bookshops in Nairobi they were all doing their own importation. There was a place for a wholesale distribution outlet for books. After further visits by myself, Phil Burnham and Neil

Wardrope it was decided to go ahead with starting a wholesale distribution operation in Kenya.

Meanwhile we closed down the operation in Chesterfield and I took a desk in the IO in Sheffield. Like most things in mission the biggest handicap to innovation was finance and CLC put £2,000 in an account for me to use. How then to proceed.

When I considered who would benefit most apart from the readers of the books and I concluded that publishers who had no representation in East Africa may be interested in supporting this effort. I approached major publishers in UK and USA and managed to persuade 20 publishers to give us 2 or 3 thousand pounds either as cash or in stock and to give us the best possible trade terms. We placed orders to be consolidated and shipped to Kenya.

Next job was to recruit a team, train them and find premises. So yet another trip to Kenya. During previous visits we had advertised that we were looking for staff so it was arranged to interview those we had shortlisted. One of the candidates stood out head and shoulders above the others and we appointed Edith Wamalwa as the manager.

When we met a few weeks later for our first staff meeting we still had no premises and met in the guest house garden. We then borrowed the use of an office from the Anglican church and started training and searching for premises.

Eventually we found a great premise at the White House, Gitanga Road, by Valley Arcade. We fitted out a storage facility and set up a retail shop area as well. We had to increase our staff as we needed someone to live on the premises for security reasons. The young man we offered that job came to us very few days after he had started and gave us his notice. He had been offered a far better job with real prospects, so we sent him off with our blessing. But we needed someone quickly. A local pastor recommended a fellow who came down and started working straight away. We needed to pay him straight away and for the next few weeks we had to extend times between payments to stretch out to regular weekly payments. Albert came from one of the largest slum areas in Africa in Kawangwara. Albert was a literal tower of strength for us, especially during a period of civil unrest. Unfortunately some years later we had to part company as he succumbed to temptation in a typical African way.

Over the next few years we extended our business by opening shops in Umoja, Eldoret and also Kakamega It was a constant challenge to develop new product ranges and extend our customer base. We had a stand at the Nairobi bookfair every year.

One year I saw an advertisement in the paper in UK by British Airways saying that they were working with the UK government to help develop export business by offering free flights to trade fares with a number of other benefits included. Assuming that as a charity we would be ineligible I didn't follow up until the advert was repeated a few weeks later. I then applied and went through the process of selection before being told that we would be supported to attend the Nairobi Bookfair. The government paid for the fittings for the display stand (that we continued using for some time after the fair) They paid for us to airfreight product from UK for use at the fair. And they gave a business class flight for me to attend. It was the only time I got upgraded in all my travels around Africa over the years.

In the last chapter I mentioned that I had travelled to Dar-es-Salaam, in Tanzania for the opening of that shop. Some years later the shop was struggling and I was asked to visit whilst in Nairobi to offer support and consultancy. Tanzania had not been set up on strong foundations and some of the original staffing had left, leaving the present Manager who had health problems in a difficult situation. Over a couple of years I visited Tanzania on several occasions.

Those who know Africa will be aware that ethical morality is looked at differently by some, even those who are Christians. From time to time this led to difficult decisions. On one occasion Neil Wardrope and Liz Patten (African regional director) visited our shop in Swaziland only to find that the shop was virtually empty of stock and on investigation very little money in the bank. It was obvious that there had been some misappropriation by someone on the staff. On their return to UK I was asked to consider taking a trip to Manzini to see if we could rescue the situation. I visited on several occasions but the decision was eventually taken to close that shop. Some of this was due to local pressures but also to the general changes in the worldwide book business.

I had been struggling with life for some time and in 2009/10 I had to take an extended period off work, I started to get some counselling but found it of little benefit. When I returned to work it was on reduced hours and I felt that overseas travel was not going to be feasible. So what to do?

I helped with a number of projects in the International Office. Finding and entering data on to software systems for the various fields around the world. I helped produce buying lists of suitable books for bookstalls at some international conferences.

One major project we started was to develop online training courses for new recruits in English speaking countries of CLC. It was a completely new area for me and very interesting. Along with this I wrote a handbook for new recruits both to CLC and in any Christian bookshop. Compatible with this I wrote a book for managers that was similar but in greater depth. When I attended the CLC International Conference in Panama, these books were taken up and subsequently translated into Spanish.

September 2015 came round and I was able to retire. For those approaching retirement may I suggest that you plan what you are going to do as I completed my plans in about 3 days.

The astute reader will have noticed less mention of Isobel as we had really drifted apart. She was busy with her activities, and I found time sitting heavy. One thing I did do was volunteer with Derbyshire Police. As a police volunteer we assisted police in areas that civilians were able to. We helped with role playing for training, Running the Video Links for remote attendance at courts by police and witnesses, Helping with searching for Missing persons etc. It was really worthwhile and great fun. If we had stayed in the area I would have continued as long as I could.

After university in Edinburgh, Becki had stayed in Scotland and had moved into a flat in Stirling. Mark had attended university in Stirling and stayed in Scotland particularly in Edinburgh, After University in Sheffield, Tim moved up to Stirling and shared flat with Becki. Isobel and I realised that the house we were renting was now too large, it also suffered from damp and too many stairs. So we started to look for somewhere else, Isobel wanted to move back to Scotland where most of her family still lived. We took time to look for a property that was convenient for both Stirling and Edinburgh, but that was not on the doorstep of any of the kids. We should have remembered that people who move to live near their kids will find that the kids then move away. In our case one to China and the other to USA.

Chapter18

TILLICOULTRY - THE END OF THE ROAD? 2017 –

August 12th 2017 we move to Kirkhill Terrace, in Tillicoultry. The day of the move was horrendous, but I had a hope that we could make a fresh start in Tilly. The house was a lot smaller than we lived in previously, so we had disposed of a lot of stuff. It seemed to my mind that we still had a lot that we didn't need. Most of the stuff was stacked in the living room and spare bedroom and the removal men had gone. It took us weeks to get the house in a semblance of order, I was treading on eggshells to not argue but we even had long discussions about where the furniture would go, even though there was, in my mind, only one obvious place.

Isobel started to go to a church in Stirling so left early Sunday morning and would come back somewhen. She soon got involved in other activities and would be out all day and sometimes late in the evening. I had found out about the Men's Shed movement and got involved with the branch in Tilly. I was able to do some practical tasks for the house and got involved with other projects as well. It was great to get out of the house 3 days a week to enjoy some banter and be active with a great bunch of guys. I also attended the Tilly Baptist church meetings at the local community hall. Just as we arrived in Tilly the roof of the church had collapsed, and they had to move out temporarily.

The Pastor of the church, Pete Foster, was an ex-OM ships man and he and I got on well, he was a good sounding board. But I never really felt welcomed so after a while I stopped going.

For a while life seemed to settle down. We had Christmas together with Becki, Mark and Katya and Tim all together which was the last time we were all together. Things continued but relations were strained It seemed to me. Isobel had stopped doing anything more than the absolute basics for me. I was doing my own laundry, cooking most of my own meals and spending most of the time alone.

In October 2018 Ruth and Peter treated us to a holiday on the Isle of Wight, Alan and Susan, and Beryl and Sharon were also there as a siblings get together. Of the 5 days we were there Isobel spent 3 of the days with a friend who lived on the island. On the last day we heard that Mark was unhappy and the next day we heard that He and Katya had separated so we drove straight back to see him in Edinburgh. We found him in a poor state, hungry and homeless so it was obvious that he came and stayed with us. He lived with us for several weeks, working in Edinburgh until he found a flat share near where he worked. Then Christmas was on us again.

Almost straight away we were back to normal and I didn't know where I stood. I was at home one Monday evening thinking that Isobel had missed the last bus home from Stirling. She came in and after a few minutes came and said that she was leaving the next morning. Which she did. She had her reasons, which we had discussed but I felt and still do that they were insufficient grounds for separation.

I was left living in a house alone. My Pension and benefits reduced from being for a couple to being for a single person, so I could no longer afford the rent on the house. Since my breakdown, told about in the last chapter, Isobel had organised all the bill payments etc. and I now had to deal with that. I seriously considered suicide but got little further than considering it. I had a couple of sessions with Pete Foster that was very helpful, but still could see no future, What's the point. Pete was on Sabbatical when I decided to try the church again and went along on a couple of Sunday mornings and sat on the back row, sometimes in tears but apart from a handshake at the door nobody spoke to me. Then on one Sunday I went in sat through the service and walked out without anyone speaking to me. I was so emotional/angry/upset that I walked back in and spoke to the person on the sound desk, (nearest to the door) and said how bad I thought it was that someone could come to a service, and no one spoke to them. At this point an elderly lady actually said "I think you had better leave I've got my stick with me you know" I just walked out. When I got home, I sat and sent an email to the Church Secretary saying how I felt. Bless him, Frank Kremer took the time and trouble to help put me in touch with others.

I was invited to join the Thursday walking group, which is less a walking group than an older group social gathering for coffee after a stroll. It gave me an opportunity to meet some folks at church and to get to know them. I gradually got more and more involved with the church. I started to attend a house group during the summer of 2019 and got to know the group. They have been a real blessing to me and are some of my closest friends. The studies we did challenged me and have changed me as I allowed the teaching to influence my thinking. I believe that I am a better person for it.

Pete resigned and moved to a church some miles away, so the church was left without a Pastor. The Elders took up the challenge and have drawn the church together and not only maintained what we do but has encouraged growth and development. I was asked to consider joining the fellowship which I was privileged to do in November 2019. As the church started to look for a new Pastor we have been hit by the Corona Virus. What differences will that make to the church and the way we and other churches operate and survive or thrive. We will see what God has got in hand for us as a Church in the remainder of 2020.

Since I wrote this in 2020, the church have found a new pastor, Dee Jess, and we have been blessed to see the church grow. As of 2024 we are in the process of redeveloping a larger church building to facilitate the growth.

Chapter 19

NEARLY BUT NOT QUITE

When I dusted the metaphorical cobwebs off this manuscript what did I want it to say, who had I written it for. Yes, there are some mildly funny anecdotes and stories there are interesting and unique times but who would be interested. I hope my own children, and if they have children my grandchildren might be interested in what the old man did. But I cannot imagine anyone else being interested in an unknown less than successful person.

As you will realise from the chapter titles, I have a great interest in places as well as people. During the course of this little book, I visited 51 different countries plus a few where I only saw the airport. I have had 37 different postal addresses. Apart from the UK I have lived and worked in 3 other countries for at least 3 months. I have been privileged to meet some great and famous people but more importantly I have met and am friends with some truly awesome ordinary people.

If you have read this far you will realise that I never achieved very much. I nearly succeeded at many things but NOT QUITE. Could I have worked harder at school and passed my exams, with a view to university and a completely different life? Could I have tried harder in the Navy? who knows I might have managed to last long enough to get a pension, a commission or even both. Could I have stuck it out at Bentleys' and taken a senior job there and a career in purchasing? I might have worked harder at my 1st marriage and had a satisfied wife still by my side. But I didn't. Some would say I was a failure at that point.

From a low point there I managed to claw my way back up. It was suggested that I stay on with OM when my time was up, but circumstances were against it. Might I have ended up in leadership there, if that is success? Could it have been that I rose to a senior position in the Christian book trade. By the worlds standards I did OK but didn't quite make it to the top. Nearly but not Quite.

What are the lessons I have learnt from this process. I know its near enough to the end to skip this bit and pick up another book.

We are not always in control of the circumstances around us and sometimes they are the cause of our failure or feeling of failure. We often make the decision we do because it is the obvious one in front of us. Sometimes this leads to failure. But really the measure of success or failure is not on how high we get up the corporate ladder or in the size of the deals we do but, on the regularity, and consistency of the good that we do.

But above all I have learned that whatever happens, God is with me. He is able to achieve His purposes using weak and faulty vessels like me. That our success is not what we achieve in the eyes of the world. Success is when we give thanks for the redeeming work of the Lord Jesus Christ, we allow the Holy Spirit to empower our lives so that we can Love and serve God to the best of our ability.

I can only say that although I often failed He never does.

v1 I will exalt you, Lord, for you lifted me out of the depths and did not let my enemies gloat over me.

v2 Lord my God, I called to you for help, and you healed me.

v3 You, Lord, brought me up from the realm of the dead; you spared me from going down to the pit.

v4 Sing the praises of the Lord, you his faithful people: praise his holy name

Psalms 30 v 1-4 ESV

Not that I have already obtained this or am already perfect, but I press on to make it my own, because Christ Jesus has made me his own. Brothers, I do not consider that I have made it my own. But one thing I do: forgetting what lies behind and straining forward to what lies ahead, I press on toward the goal for the prize of the upward call of God in Christ Jesus

Philippians ch3 v 12-14

These were the verses my father highlighted in the New Testament he gave me on the day I joined the Royal Navy

Printed in Great Britain
by Amazon